Risk Stability

How to Control Exposure, Limit Downside, and Stay Financially Stable

Mark Ellison

PERENNIAL PUBLISHING

Published by Perennial Publishing

First Edition

Paperback ISBN: 978-1-971996-27-1
Hardcover ISBN: 978-1-971996-28-8
EBook ISBN: 978-1-971996-29-5

For bulk or institutional orders, contact Perennial Publishing.

Contents

Stability as a Structural Condition

Stability is commonly understood through its visible surface. A system is called stable when outcomes appear smooth, when disruption is absent, when obligations are met without visible strain, and when operations continue without interruption. Under this view, stability is inferred from calm. If nothing appears to be failing, the system is treated as sound. If outcomes remain orderly, the structure beneath them is assumed to be durable. This interpretation is widespread because it aligns with what can be observed directly. What is visible is continuity, so continuity is treated as proof of resilience. What is absent is disruption, so absence is treated as evidence of safety.

That interpretation is limited from the beginning. Smooth outcomes do not necessarily indicate structural strength. They may indicate that the system has not yet been tested in a way that exposes its limits. A structure can appear stable because conditions have remained favorable enough that its vulnerabilities have not yet been activated. It may continue operating inside a narrow band of tolerance without revealing how little variation it can actually absorb. In such cases, calm does not confirm robustness. It confirms only that the conditions required to expose fragility have not yet arrived. The appearance of stability and the existence of stability are therefore not identical.

This distinction between observed calm and structural stability defines the central reorientation of this book. Stability cannot be understood only through visible outcomes because outcomes are often delayed expressions of prior conditions. What appears orderly at the surface may rest on concentrated dependency, compressed margin, or narrow timing alignment that remains invisible until some disturbance forces those conditions into view. The absence of visible failure does not confirm strength. It confirms only that failure has not yet become visible. Structural stability must therefore be assessed beneath outcomes rather than inferred from them.

This requires a second shift. Events do not create failure in the strong sense often assumed. They reveal it. A disruption may look like the cause of instability because it is the moment at which strain becomes visible, but visibility is not origin. When a system breaks under pressure, the break does not arise from the event alone. It arises from the interaction between the event and the structure receiving it. Dependency, fragility, timing sensitivity, and limited capacity all exist before disruption appears. The event exposes those conditions by forcing the system to respond under circumstances where its underlying structure can no longer remain hidden.

This reframing matters because it moves explanation away from event magnitude alone. The same disturbance can produce different outcomes in different systems because the event is not the full explanation. One structure absorbs what another transmits. One system remains continuous while another destabilizes. If the event were sufficient as explanation, similar events would produce similar outcomes across contexts. They do not. What differs is the configuration that receives the event. Failure therefore follows structure more than event category. External disturbance matters, but it matters through the architecture it enters.

The distinction, then, is between cause and revelation. In ordinary interpretation, the event is treated as the cause and the system as the passive recipient. In structural interpretation, the event is the revealing condition. It forces existing properties into expression. A disruption can expose dependency that was previously latent, timing constraints that were previously manageable, or limited tolerance that had not yet been measured. This does not reduce the significance of events. It repositions them. Events are the conditions under which structure becomes legible. They do not explain the system alone. They expose how the system was built before they arrived.

Once this shift is made, risk must also be understood differently. Risk is often treated as episodic, as if it appears when events occur and disappears when they do not. Under that model, systems move between risk and safety according to what is immediately happening around them. Calm periods are treated as low-risk periods because nothing visible is wrong. Stress periods are treated as high-risk periods because visible disturbance has arrived. This model is intuitive because it aligns risk with observation. But structurally, it is incomplete.

Exposure is continuous. Systems operate under it at all times. Risk does not begin when an event occurs. It exists beforehand as the condition that makes consequences possible when events do occur. A system may carry concentrated dependence, narrow flexibility, timing mismatch, or constrained capacity long before any outward sign of instability appears. These are not temporary states that switch on only in crisis. They are ongoing structural conditions. Risk therefore exists before events, between events, and regardless of whether it is currently visible in outcomes.

This distinction between episodic risk and continuous exposure is foundational. It means systems are never genuinely risk-free in the structural sense. They are operating under exposure at all times, with the only difference being whether that exposure is currently activated into visible consequence. A stable system is not a system without exposure. It is a system whose exposure remains within a range that can be absorbed without structural breakdown. Stability must therefore be understood as a condition under ongoing exposure, not as a temporary exemption from it. Systems do not move between safe and unsafe states in a simple binary sequence. They operate continuously inside exposure, and what changes is whether that exposure remains contained.

If exposure is continuous, then outcomes must be governed by structural conditions that persist beneath visible events. Configuration matters because it determines how much continuity depends on how many supports. Dependencies matter because they determine which components rely on which others. Capacity matters because it determines how much variation can be absorbed before strain becomes consequential. Timing matters because even sufficient resources can fail to stabilize a system if they arrive or must be used in the wrong sequence. These conditions are not secondary details surrounding events. They are the primary determinants of how the system behaves once events occur.

Structure defines whether disruption is absorbed locally, transmitted across connected components, or amplified into larger consequence. It determines whether stress remains within normal operating range or moves the system toward instability. A system with wider margin and better-aligned support behaves differently under the same disturbance than one operating near its limits. A system with distributed dependencies behaves differently than one concentrated around a small number of critical points. External variability interacts with internal design. It does not replace it. This is why system behavior under stress cannot be understood from events alone. Structure governs the meaning of those events.

Surface-level analysis often obscures this. It focuses on what became visible after an outcome occurred. It identifies the failure point, the loss event, the timing of a disruption, or the immediate source of pressure. This kind of analysis can explain symptoms. It can describe the visible sequence by which breakdown became apparent. But it often remains too close to the surface to identify the deeper conditions that allowed the outcome to become possible. It explains manifestation more easily than architecture.

This is the distinction between observational explanation and structural explanation. Observational explanation tracks what happened. Structural explanation asks what conditions made that result possible, transmissible, or irreversible. The first is often temporally late. It begins where visibility begins. The second begins earlier, in the arrangement of dependencies, capacities, and timing relationships that were already in place before the visible outcome occurred. What is visible is frequently the final stage of a longer process. By the time instability is clearly observable, much of the structural development that made it possible may already be complete.

For that reason, systems must be understood beneath their visible behavior. The operating surface is informative, but incomplete. A structure may appear smooth because pressure is still being absorbed silently. It may appear strong because no recent event has been large enough to test its limits. It may appear diversified because categories differ on paper while depending on the same underlying support conditions. Surface analysis therefore produces partial understanding. It captures the symptoms of system behavior but often misses the mechanisms that generate those symptoms. This book begins from the position that structural explanation is necessary if stability is to be understood at all.

That understanding also requires recognizing that systems operate within boundaries. Stability is not open-ended. A system remains stable only while conditions remain inside the range it can absorb. Within that range, variation can be contained. Timing can remain manageable. Disturbance can be processed without reorganizing the system into a more dangerous state. Beyond that range, instability emerges. The system does not simply become slightly more stressed. It begins behaving according to different rules because the conditions that previously allowed absorption no longer hold.

This distinction between continuous operation and bounded operation is critical. Systems can continue functioning for long periods whi
remaining closer to their limits than their outward behavior sugge

harmless. Then, once a limit is engaged or a revealing disturbance occurs, expression becomes rapid. The visible phase looks abrupt because the structural phase was largely hidden.

This is the distinction between development and expression. Failure is frequently the visible result of prior accumulation rather than a new condition appearing without preparation. Sudden outcomes often have long structural origins. By the time breakdown is visible, much of the process that made it possible has already occurred. This is why event-focused interpretation is so often incomplete. It begins at the point where instability becomes observable, not at the point where instability began to form. System thinking must therefore include latent development, not only visible activation.

At this point, the central shift of the book can be stated directly. Event thinking asks, "What happened?" System thinking asks, "What allowed this to happen?" The first question is reactive. It begins with visible disruption and tries to account for it after the fact. The second is structural. It begins with architecture, dependencies, and mechanisms, then asks how those conditions would behave under strain. This book operates within the second frame. It is not organized around isolated events, but around the recurring structural patterns through which systems absorb, transmit, or amplify disturbance.

This distinction between reactive explanation and structural understanding defines the scope of what follows. Events are still relevant, but they are treated as entry points rather than explanations. They reveal system properties. They do not, by themselves, explain why some systems remain stable while others destabilize. Understanding stability requires analyzing system architecture, because architecture determines how exposure behaves when activated. That is the analytic shift this introduction is intended to establish.

The book's purpose follows from that shift. It does not prescribe behavior, provide tactical steps, or offer optimization formulas for immediate application. It analyzes structural mechanisms of stability. It examines how systems absorb disruption, how they fail to absorb it, how instability develops beneath calm conditions, and how visible outcomes arise from earlier structural processes. The goal is understanding, not direction. The book is built to clarify what stability is, how it operates, and why it cannot be reduced to visible calm or recent continuity alone.

This is why mechanisms are the unit of analysis. A concept can name a condition, but a mechanism explains how that condition behaves. Mechanisms are recurring structural patterns that make system outcomes intelligible across contexts. They are not one-time observations or isolated abstractions. They describe repeatable relationships between exposure, structure, timing, dependency, and consequence. Each chapter isolates a mechanism not to treat it as fully independent, but to make its role in the broader system visible with precision.

The difference between concepts and mechanisms matters here. Concepts describe. Mechanisms explain. A concept may tell the reader that fragility exists, that exposure matters, or that timing is important. A mechanism shows how fragility becomes visible, how exposure translates into consequence, or how timing alters system behavior under pressure. This book is therefore organized mechanism by mechanism because structural understanding requires explanatory units that can operate across contexts and interact without collapsing into generality. The system is built from interacting mechanisms, and those mechanisms provide the repeatable explanatory structure the rest of the book will develop.

The final orientation is therefore clear. Stability is not an outcome. It is not a state achieved once. It is not the absence of disruption. Stability is structural. It is conditional. It exists only so long as the system remains configured in a way that can absorb what arrives without allowing that pressure to reorganize the system into breakdown. A stable system is not one to which nothing happens. It is one whose structure is able to absorb what does happen without losing continuity.

Stability is not determined by what happens to a system, but by how the system is structured to absorb what happens.

The Event Illusion Mechanism

Risk is misinterpreted when framed as isolated events.

The Event Illusion Mechanism describes a structural error in how risk is located and interpreted within a system. It arises when discrete occurrences are treated as the primary carriers of instability, displacing attention away from the underlying configuration that determines how those occurrences are absorbed. It does not deny the existence of events or their effects. It isolates a misalignment between what is observed and what is causal. Events are visible, bounded, and temporally precise, which allows them to dominate explanation. The system's condition, by contrast, is continuous, embedded, and less directly observable, which allows it to remain implicit. The illusion is sustained when the visible is treated as sufficient explanation, and the embedded is treated as secondary context.

An event is a discrete interruption in the continuity of a system. It is identifiable, temporally bounded, and externally observable. It occurs at a point or within a defined interval and produces a measurable deviation from a prior state. Events are episodic by definition. They emerge, register, and resolve within a timeframe that allows them to be isolated from the surrounding continuity. Because they are bounded, they can be cataloged, compared, and sequenced. This boundedness is what makes events analytically attractive, but it also restricts their explanatory capacity to the moment of occurrence.

A condition is not bounded in the same way. It is a persistent state that exists across time, independent of whether it is currently being activated by an event. Conditions do not begin or end at identifiable moments; they persist as the underlying environment within which events occur. A system's condition includes its structural arrangement, its constraints, its margins, and its internal dependencies. These elements do not appear only when an event occurs; they exist continuously and shape the system's behavior even in the absence of disruption. A condition is therefore not an occurrence but a state of being that determines how occurrences will be processed.

Exposure is a specific expression of condition. It represents the system's sensitivity to a particular class of disturbances. Exposure is not the disturbance itself, nor is it the outcome of that disturbance. It is the relationship between the system's configuration and the potential for that configuration to be affected by external or internal variation. Exposure is embedded in how tightly elements are coupled, how much buffer exists between load and capacity, how dependent the system is on uninterrupted inputs, and how quickly it can adjust when those inputs change. It is continuous and latent, present regardless of whether it is currently being activated by an event.

The distinction between event, condition, and exposure establishes the conceptual boundary necessary for accurate risk interpretation. An event is a trigger that activates interaction. A condition is the persistent state that exists before and after that interaction. Exposure is the system's sensitivity within that state, determining how the interaction will propagate. When these are conflated, the trigger is mistaken for the source, and the system's embedded properties are displaced from analysis. The Event Illusion Mechanism operates precisely at this point of conflation, where the bounded is mistaken for the causal, and the continuous is treated as background.

Events receive disproportionate explanatory weight because they are aligned with how perception organizes information. Visibility is the first driver. Events produce observable change, and observable change demands explanation. The system's condition, being continuous, does not produce discrete signals that call attention to itself. It remains stable in appearance even when it carries significant exposure. The analytical process is therefore drawn toward what changes rather than what persists. Visibility concentrates attention on the moment of disruption and away from the continuity that made the disruption consequential.

Timing reinforces this concentration. Events occur at identifiable points, allowing them to be placed in sequence relative to outcomes. This sequencing creates a temporal alignment that suggests causality. The event precedes the outcome, and this precedence is interpreted as explanatory. The system's condition, lacking a clear start or end point, cannot be sequenced in the same way. It does not present itself as a moment that can be placed before an outcome. As a result, it is excluded from the primary causal chain, even though it is the element that determines how the event will be processed.

Narrative bias completes the weighting. Events can be described in a linear structure: an occurrence followed by a consequence. This structure aligns with how explanations are constructed. It allows for clear attribution and coherent storytelling. Conditions and exposures do not fit this structure. They require continuous description rather than discrete sequencing. They do not provide a natural beginning or end, which makes them less compatible with narrative explanation. As a result, they are often omitted or simplified, and the event absorbs the explanatory role by default.

This disproportionate weighting produces a systematic distortion. The system is interpreted through the lens of its interruptions rather than through the structure that governs those interruptions. Events become explanatory anchors, and the system's condition becomes contextual background. The more this pattern is repeated, the more the Event Illusion Mechanism stabilizes as the default mode of interpretation. The system's embedded properties remain unexamined because they do not present themselves as discrete explanatory units.

When explanation is anchored to events, systems are interpreted backward from the point of disruption. The outcome is observed first, followed by the identification of the event that preceded it. This backward construction compresses the analytical timeline. The moment of occurrence becomes the origin point, and the system's prior state is treated as secondary. The internal configuration is then interpreted only in relation to the event, rather than as an independent determinant of risk. This inversion shifts causality from structure to occurrence.

The backward interpretation introduces a structural error. It assumes that the event initiated the condition that produced the outcome. In reality, the condition existed prior to the event and determined how the event would propagate. The event did not create the system's exposure; it intersected with it. By interpreting backward, the system's pre-existing configuration is obscured. The analysis begins at the point where the system is already interacting with the event, rather than at the point where the system's capacity to absorb that event was established.

This misinterpretation can be examined through the behavior of repeated disruptions. When different events produce similar outcomes, the backward interpretation attributes each outcome to its respective event. The pattern is fragmented into separate explanations. However, the consistency of outcomes indicates a stable underlying exposure. The system is positioned in a way that amplifies a range of disturbances, and this positioning persists across events. The backward interpretation fails to identify this continuity because it resets the analysis at each occurrence.

The structural consequence of this error is that the system is not evaluated in its own right. It is evaluated only as a receiver of events. Its configuration is not treated as a source of risk but as a context in which risk materializes. This prevents the identification of embedded vulnerabilities that exist independently of any specific occurrence. The system appears stable in the absence of events, even when it carries significant exposure, because the analysis has no mechanism for recognizing risk outside of disruption.

The distinction between continuous exposure and discrete disruption becomes critical in resolving this misinterpretation. Exposure is continuous. It exists at all times as a property of the system's configuration. It does not appear or disappear with events. It persists across intervals, shaping how the system will respond whenever a disturbance occurs. Disruption, by contrast, is discrete. It occurs at specific moments and interacts with the system's exposure at those moments. The interaction produces an outcome, but the exposure that determined that outcome was present before the disruption and remains after it.

When risk is framed through discrete disruption, it appears intermittent. It seems to emerge when events occur and to recede when they do not. This framing creates the impression that the system is stable between disruptions. However, this impression is a function of visibility, not of structure. The system's exposure remains unchanged during these intervals. The absence of disruption does not indicate the absence of risk; it indicates that the system has not recently encountered a trigger that intersects with its exposure in a destabilizing way.

At the point where continuous exposure and discrete disruption are clearly separated, the structural difference between event-based and exposure-based models becomes visible.

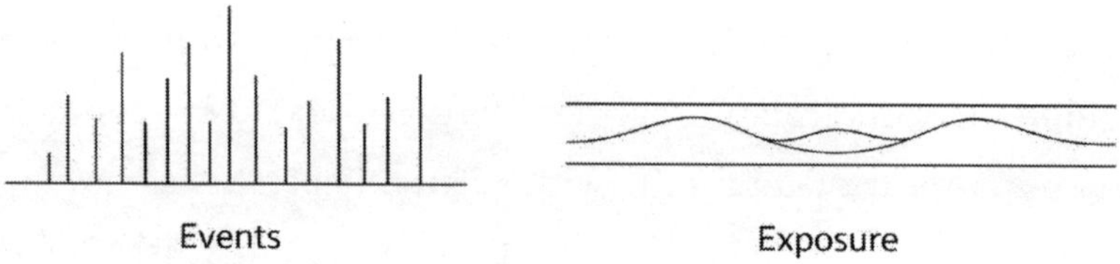

[Figure 1: Event vs Exposure Model]

The figure clarifies that in an event-based model, risk is mapped to discrete occurrences. The system is represented as stable between these occurrences, with risk appearing only at the moment of disruption. In an exposure-based model, risk is mapped to the system's continuous configuration. Events are depicted as intersections that reveal how that configuration behaves under stress. The same event produces different outcomes depending on the underlying exposure, demonstrating that the event is not the determinant of risk but the mechanism through which exposure is expressed.

The misclassification between episodic and embedded risk follows from this distinction. Episodic risk is defined as risk that exists only during events. It is treated as an external force that intermittently affects the system. Embedded risk, by contrast, is a property of the system itself. It exists continuously, regardless of whether it is currently being activated. When risk is misclassified as episodic, the system's exposure is effectively removed from analysis. Stability is inferred from the absence of events, and vulnerability is associated only with their presence.

This misclassification produces a structural blind spot. A system with high embedded exposure can appear stable for extended periods if no triggering events occur. During these periods, the system accumulates no visible evidence of risk, reinforcing the perception of stability. When a disruption eventually occurs, the resulting instability is attributed to the event, rather than to the exposure that made the system sensitive to it. The cycle then repeats, with each event reinforcing the episodic classification and further obscuring the embedded nature of risk.

The distinction between episodic and embedded risk also affects how variability is interpreted. In an episodic frame, variability is seen as a sequence of independent disturbances. Each event is treated as a separate instance, with its own cause and effect. In an embedded frame, variability is understood as a continuous interaction between exposure and a range of potential disturbances. The system's behavior is not a series of isolated reactions but a consistent expression of its configuration under different conditions. The episodic frame fragments this continuity, while the embedded frame preserves it.

The structural consequence of this misclassification is a shift in system orientation. When risk is treated as episodic, the system becomes reactive. Attention is directed toward identifying and responding to events as they occur. The analytical process is anchored to disruption, and adjustments are made in response to observed outcomes. Because the underlying exposure is not treated as the primary variable, these adjustments do not alter the system's structural sensitivity. The system remains configured in the same way, and similar outcomes emerge when different events interact with it.

In contrast, when risk is understood as embedded, the system's orientation becomes anticipatory in a structural sense. The focus is not on predicting specific events but on recognizing the continuous exposure that exists within the system. Analysis is directed toward the configuration itself—its constraints, its buffers, its dependencies—and how these elements determine the system's capacity to absorb variation. Events are incorporated as tests of this configuration, not as the origin of risk. The system is evaluated based on its positioning relative to potential disturbances, rather than on its history of interactions with them.

The divergence between reactive and anticipatory orientations extends across time. A reactive system continually adjusts in response to events, without altering the underlying exposure that generates those responses. Over time, this produces a pattern of repeated instability, where different events trigger similar outcomes. An anticipatory system, by contrast, evaluates and adjusts its configuration in recognition of continuous exposure. This alters how the system will respond to future disturbances, even if those disturbances are not specifically identified in advance. The difference is not in the frequency of events but in how the system is positioned to absorb them.

As the progression develops, the distinction between occurrence and condition becomes the central point of transition. If events are triggers and exposure is continuous, then risk cannot be accurately located in occurrences. Occurrences activate interaction, but they do not define the system's sensitivity to that interaction. The system's condition—its configuration, its constraints, its exposure—exists independently of any specific event and determines how any event will propagate. Risk, therefore, must be understood as a condition of the system rather than as an attribute of isolated events.

This transition resolves the distortion introduced by the Event Illusion Mechanism. It separates the visible from the causal and repositions analysis from discrete moments to continuous structure. Events remain part of the system's operation, but their role is redefined. They are not sources of risk but points of interaction that reveal the system's embedded properties. The system's condition becomes the primary object of analysis, and risk is understood as a continuous property of that condition, present at all times and expressed through the events that intersect with it.

The Exposure vs Probability Mechanism

The Exposure vs Probability Mechanism defines a structural separation between two variables that are routinely conflated: likelihood and consequence. Likelihood refers to the probability that an event occurs within a given interval. It is a measure of frequency, expressed as a rate or chance of occurrence. Consequence refers to the magnitude of impact when that event does occur. It is a measure of system disturbance, expressed as loss, disruption, or structural displacement. These variables operate on independent axes. Probability determines whether an event appears often; consequence determines whether an event matters when it appears. The mechanism exists to prevent the collapse of these dimensions into a single evaluative frame, because once they are collapsed, systems begin to optimize for the wrong variable.

At a surface level, the distinction appears straightforward. An event can be rare but severe, or frequent but minor. However, the structural behavior of systems depends not on recognizing this distinction in abstraction, but on maintaining it in configuration. When likelihood and consequence are not separated, probability becomes a proxy for importance. Events that occur frequently are treated as structurally significant, regardless of their limited impact, while events that occur infrequently are discounted, regardless of their potential to destabilize the system. The mechanism therefore begins by enforcing a dimensional boundary: probability answers the question of occurrence; consequence answers the question of impact. No translation exists between them without introducing distortion.

As systems operate over time, this separation becomes more critical rather than less. Probability accumulates as repeated observation. Consequence accumulates as irreversible change. The system does not experience probability directly; it experiences outcomes. Yet the system often evaluates itself using probability metrics, because they are more readily observable. This creates a persistent structural asymmetry: the variable that is easiest to measure becomes the variable that dominates decision weighting, even if it is not the variable that determines system stability.

Probability dominates perception because it presents itself through frequency, measurability, and cognitive accessibility. Frequency creates visibility. Events that occur often generate repeated signals, reinforcing their presence within the system's observational field. Measurability provides numerical clarity. Probability can be expressed as percentages, rates, or distributions, allowing it to be compared, ranked, and tracked. Cognitive weighting follows from repetition and quantification. The system assigns importance to what it sees often and can measure precisely, because these attributes create the appearance of control.

This dominance is not incidental; it is structurally reinforced over time. Each cycle of observation strengthens the association between frequency and relevance. High-probability events generate continuous feedback loops. They appear in data, in monitoring systems, and in immediate experience. As a result, the system calibrates its attention toward these events, allocating resources, adjustments, and analysis capacity in proportion to their visibility. This creates a self-reinforcing loop: the more an event is observed, the more it is measured; the more it is measured, the more it is treated as significant; the more it is treated as significant, the more attention it receives in subsequent cycles.

However, this dominance does not extend to outcome severity. Probability determines how often an event occurs, but it does not determine the scale of disruption when it does occur. A high-probability event can produce negligible structural change, while a low-probability event can produce irreversible system displacement. The two variables do not correlate in magnitude. Probability operates on frequency; consequence operates on scale. When the system uses probability as a proxy for impact, it introduces a distortion that systematically underestimates low-frequency, high-impact events.

This distortion becomes more pronounced across multiple cycles. Because high-probability events are continuously observed, they create the illusion of cumulative importance. The system experiences them repeatedly and begins to associate repetition with risk. Meanwhile, low-probability events remain absent from immediate observation. Their absence is interpreted as irrelevance rather than as latent exposure. Over time, the system constructs a model in which risk is defined by frequency alone. This model is stable under normal conditions, because high-frequency events dominate day-to-day experience. It fails under stress, because the events that generate system-level disruption are not the ones that occur most often.

Exposure introduces the structural variable that determines impact when events occur. Exposure is not the probability of an event, but the degree to which the system is affected if that event materializes. It is defined by the amount of system capacity, resource allocation, or structural dependency that is positioned within the path of the event. Exposure converts an event from a possibility into a potential disturbance. Without exposure, probability has no consequence. With exposure, even a low-probability event can generate significant impact.

At a first level, exposure can be understood as magnitude of vulnerability. It measures how much of the system is at stake. However, this definition remains incomplete without considering how exposure is embedded within system configuration. Exposure is not a static quantity; it is a function of how resources, obligations, and dependencies are arranged. Two systems can face the same probabilistic environment but experience different outcomes because their exposure profiles differ. The mechanism therefore shifts evaluation from external likelihood to internal configuration. It asks not how often an event occurs, but how much of the system is affected when it does.

Structurally, exposure behaves as a multiplier of consequence. When an event occurs, its impact is scaled by the degree of exposure. A small exposure limits the disturbance to a contained portion of the system. A large exposure propagates the disturbance across multiple components, amplifying its effect. This scaling is nonlinear. As exposure increases, the system approaches thresholds where the impact transitions from manageable disruption to structural failure. These thresholds are not visible through probability analysis, because they are determined by configuration, not frequency.

The incorrect interpretation treats exposure as secondary to probability. It assumes that reducing the likelihood of events is sufficient to manage risk. Under this interpretation, systems allocate resources toward minimizing occurrence rather than controlling impact. This leads to configurations where exposure remains high because it is not directly addressed. The system becomes optimized for avoiding frequent disturbances while remaining vulnerable to infrequent ones. Over time, this creates a divergence between perceived stability and actual stability. The system appears stable because high-probability disruptions are managed, but it remains structurally fragile because exposure to low-probability events is uncontained.

Low-probability, high-exposure scenarios illustrate the consequence of this misalignment. These scenarios are characterized by events that occur rarely but intersect with large portions of the system when they do occur. Because their probability is low, they are often excluded from active consideration. They do not generate frequent signals, and they are difficult to measure with precision. As a result, they are assigned low perceptual weight. However, their exposure profile is high. When they materialize, they do not produce incremental change; they produce step-level disruption.

At a first level, these scenarios can be understood as asymmetrical risk structures. The system experiences long periods of stability punctuated by sudden, large disturbances. The absence of events during stable periods reinforces the perception that the risk is negligible. However, this absence is not indicative of low impact; it is indicative of low frequency. When the event eventually occurs, the system confronts the full magnitude of its exposure at once. The impact is not averaged over time; it is realized in a single interval.

Mechanistically, low-probability, high-exposure scenarios accumulate latent instability. Each cycle in which the event does not occur increases the system's confidence in its current configuration. This confidence often leads to further expansion of exposure, because the absence of disturbance is interpreted as validation. Over time, the system becomes more exposed precisely because the event has not occurred. When the event eventually materializes, the impact is amplified not only by the existing exposure but by the cumulative expansion of exposure during prior cycles.

The incorrect interpretation treats the rarity of these events as justification for inattention. It assumes that low probability equates to low relevance. This leads to a systematic underallocation of resources toward managing exposure. The system does not prepare for the magnitude of potential disruption because it is anchored to the frequency of occurrence. When the disruption occurs, the system is forced into reactive adjustment under compressed conditions, often at a point where the cost of adjustment is significantly higher than it would have been under proactive exposure control.

High-probability, low-exposure scenarios present the inverse structure. These scenarios occur frequently but affect only a limited portion of the system when they do occur. Their high frequency ensures that they are continuously observed and measured. They generate consistent signals, making them highly visible within the system's monitoring framework. As a result, they receive disproportionate attention relative to their actual impact.

At a first level, these scenarios can be understood as noise-dominated disturbances. They produce repeated, minor deviations that the system can absorb without significant structural change. Because their exposure is low, each occurrence results in a contained impact. The system experiences them as manageable variations rather than as threats to stability. However, their frequency creates the appearance of persistent risk. The system responds by allocating resources toward managing these events, often refining processes, controls, or buffers that address their occurrence.

Structurally, high-probability, low-exposure scenarios do not accumulate into large-scale disruption unless they are allowed to propagate through exposure expansion. Their impact remains bounded by the limited portion of the system they affect. However, the system's response to their frequency can lead to over-optimization. Resources are directed toward minimizing these events further, even though their marginal impact on overall stability is small. This creates an imbalance where the system becomes highly efficient at managing minor disturbances while remaining underprepared for major ones.

The incorrect interpretation equates frequency with severity. It assumes that because an event occurs often, it must be important. This leads to a disproportionate allocation of attention and resources toward high-probability events. Over time, the system becomes calibrated to respond to frequent, low-impact disturbances, reinforcing the perception that these events define the system's risk profile. This calibration persists across cycles, creating a stable but misaligned response pattern.

The misallocation of attention toward likelihood rather than consequence emerges from the interaction of these dynamics. Because probability is observable and measurable, it becomes the primary input for decision-making. The system constructs its model of risk based on frequency data, prioritizing events that appear often. This leads to a distribution of attention that is inversely related to actual impact. High-frequency, low-impact events receive sustained attention, while low-frequency, high-impact events are neglected.

This misallocation is not a one-time error; it is a recurring structural pattern. In each cycle, the system observes frequent events and updates its model accordingly. Because low-probability events do not appear in most cycles, they are excluded from the model. This exclusion reinforces itself. The absence of these events is interpreted as evidence of their irrelevance, further reducing the likelihood that exposure will be addressed. Meanwhile, the continuous presence of high-probability events reinforces their perceived importance, leading to additional resource allocation in their direction.

Over multiple cycles, this creates a compounding effect. The system becomes increasingly optimized for managing frequent disturbances, improving efficiency and control in areas that do not significantly affect stability. At the same time, exposure to infrequent disturbances remains unaddressed or even increases. The gap between perceived risk and actual risk widens. When a low-probability, high-exposure event eventually occurs, the system experiences a discontinuity between its expectations and its actual capacity to absorb the disturbance.

This dynamic also influences how the system adapts. Because adaptation is driven by observed events, the system evolves in response to what it sees most often. High-probability events shape the system's processes, controls, and resource allocation patterns. Low-probability events, by definition, do not contribute to this adaptive process until they occur. When they do occur, the system must adapt under conditions of stress, often making adjustments that are reactive rather than structural. This reinforces the cycle, as the system returns to focusing on high-probability events once the immediate disturbance has passed.

The mechanism therefore culminates in a structural reorientation: consequence governs system stability, not probability. Stability is determined by the magnitude of disruption the system can absorb, not by the frequency with which disturbances occur. Probability influences how often the system is tested; consequence determines whether the system remains intact after the test. When evaluation is anchored in probability, the system optimizes for avoiding frequent disturbances. When evaluation is anchored in consequence, the system configures itself to withstand impact regardless of frequency.

This reorientation does not eliminate probability; it repositions it. Probability remains relevant as a measure of occurrence, but it does not define importance. Importance is defined by consequence, which is mediated through exposure. The system must therefore evaluate events based on their potential impact given its current exposure, rather than on their likelihood of occurrence. This shifts attention from external frequency to internal configuration. It transforms risk from a question of prediction into a question of structure.

The Loss Asymmetry Mechanism

Loss asymmetry describes a structural imbalance between decline and restoration within a system. Loss and gain are not mirror processes operating on equivalent terms. A decline in system value, capacity, or position does not require an equal and opposite increase to return to the prior state. Instead, recovery demands a proportionally larger gain relative to the magnitude of the loss. This imbalance is not a behavioral artifact; it is embedded in the arithmetic and temporal structure of systems that operate on percentage change and compounding bases. When a system experiences a reduction, the base from which recovery must occur is diminished, requiring a larger relative increase to reestablish the original level.

At a first level, this can be observed through proportional relationships. A system that declines by a given percentage must recover by a greater percentage to return to its starting point. This occurs because the denominator changes after loss. The system does not recover from its original base; it recovers from a reduced base. As a result, the path back is steeper than the path down. This creates an inherent asymmetry between loss and gain that cannot be neutralized through equal percentage movements.

At a deeper level, loss asymmetry introduces a structural distortion in how systems interpret balance. When loss and gain are treated as equivalent but opposite forces, systems assume that fluctuations around a mean will self-correct over time. This assumption fails because the magnitude of recovery required increases as losses deepen. The system therefore does not oscillate symmetrically around its prior state; it drifts downward when losses occur without sufficient compensatory gain. This drift is not visible when evaluated through nominal percentage changes alone, but it becomes evident when the base-dependent nature of recovery is accounted for.

The incorrect interpretation assumes that gains offset losses in a linear fashion. Under this assumption, a system that loses and then gains the same percentage is expected to return to equilibrium. This interpretation ignores the structural dependency on base size. By treating loss and gain as symmetric, the system underestimates the recovery required and overestimates its capacity to absorb declines. This distortion becomes embedded in system evaluation, leading to configurations that tolerate losses under the assumption that they can be reversed without disproportionate effort.

Recovery requirements scale nonlinearly with loss magnitude. Small losses impose modest recovery demands because the base reduction is limited. As losses increase, the required recovery grows at an accelerating rate. This relationship is not linear because each incremental loss reduces the base further, increasing the relative gain needed to restore the system. The recovery curve therefore steepens as loss magnitude increases. The system moves from a regime where recovery is feasible within normal operating conditions to a regime where recovery requires extended time, elevated performance, or external intervention.

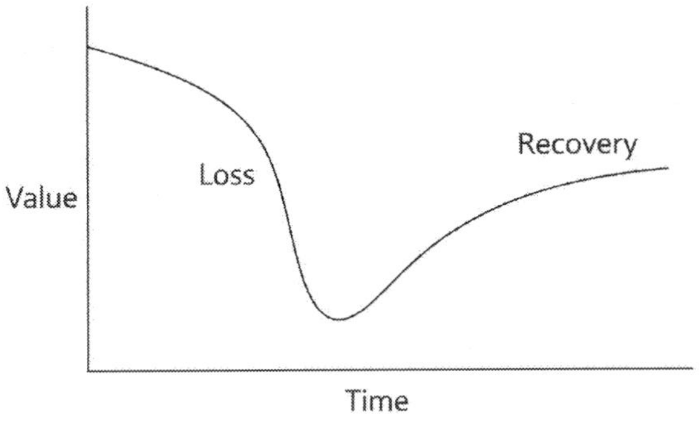

[Figure 2: Asymmetry of Loss Curve]

At a first level, the nonlinear nature of recovery can be understood through incremental scaling. A minor decline requires a slightly larger increase to recover, but the difference is small enough to be absorbed within standard variation. As the decline deepens, the gap between loss and required gain widens. The system must generate increasingly larger gains from an increasingly smaller base. This creates a compounding disadvantage, where each additional loss amplifies the recovery requirement more than proportionally.

Mechanistically, this nonlinearity introduces thresholds. Beyond certain levels of drawdown, the required recovery exceeds what the system can realistically produce within its normal operating constraints. At this point, the system transitions from recoverable to structurally impaired. The impairment is not defined by the loss itself, but by the recovery requirement exceeding feasible limits. This creates a boundary condition where further losses do not simply extend recovery time but alter the system's ability to recover at all.

The incorrect interpretation treats recovery as a linear extension of gain processes. It assumes that if a system can produce a certain rate of gain under normal conditions, it can apply that rate to recover from losses regardless of magnitude. This ignores the interaction between reduced base size and required growth rate. As losses deepen, maintaining the same rate of gain produces diminishing absolute recovery. The system appears to be improving, but the distance to the original state remains large because the base is constrained.

Over multiple cycles, nonlinear recovery requirements create divergence between systems with similar average performance but different loss profiles. A system that experiences frequent small losses and moderate gains may maintain its position, while a system that experiences occasional large losses may fail to recover despite similar average returns. The asymmetry in recovery requirements causes outcomes to diverge even when average performance metrics appear comparable. This divergence is a direct result of nonlinear scaling, not of differences in average gain.

Time introduces an additional dimension that amplifies loss asymmetry. Loss events compress time. They occur rapidly, reducing system capacity within short intervals. Gains, by contrast, accumulate over extended periods. Recovery requires sustained positive performance across multiple cycles. This creates a temporal imbalance: the time required to lose is often shorter than the time required to recover. The system experiences decline as an abrupt event and recovery as a prolonged process.

At a first level, this can be observed in the speed of change. Losses often manifest as discrete events or rapid sequences, producing immediate reductions in system state. Gains require accumulation, which is inherently gradual. The system must maintain favorable conditions over time to rebuild its position. This temporal asymmetry means that a single loss event can erase the effects of multiple periods of gain, requiring the system to reestablish those gains over an extended horizon.

Mechanistically, time compression during loss creates additional constraints. The system must absorb the decline within a limited interval, often before it can adjust its configuration. Recovery, however, requires not only time but stability during that time. The system must avoid further losses while it rebuilds, which imposes a requirement for consistent performance. Any additional disturbance during the recovery period resets or extends the recovery process, further increasing the time required.

The incorrect interpretation assumes that time operates symmetrically for loss and gain. It treats recovery as the inverse of decline, expecting that the time to recover will mirror the time to lose. This assumption fails because it ignores the accumulation requirement of gains and the base reduction caused by loss. As a result, systems underestimate the duration of recovery and overestimate their ability to return to prior states within expected timeframes.

Across multiple cycles, temporal asymmetry compounds. Each loss event introduces a recovery period that overlaps with subsequent cycles. If losses occur before recovery is complete, the system enters a state of persistent drawdown. The time required to recover extends indefinitely, and the system operates under continuous constraint. This creates a regime where recovery is not a discrete phase but a prolonged condition, reducing the system's capacity to accumulate gains.

Loss events disrupt compounding processes by reducing the base on which future growth occurs. Compounding depends on the accumulation of gains over time, with each gain building on the previous base. When a loss occurs, it removes a portion of that base, reducing the absolute amount that future gains can generate. This interruption is not temporary; it alters the trajectory of accumulation. The system does not resume compounding from its original path but from a lower starting point.

At a first level, this can be understood as a reset in growth potential. After a loss, the same rate of gain produces smaller absolute increases because it is applied to a reduced base. The system must therefore generate higher rates of gain or extend the time horizon to achieve the same absolute outcome. This creates a drag on accumulation, where progress slows relative to the pre-loss trajectory.

Mechanistically, the disruption extends beyond immediate compounding. Loss introduces secondary effects that propagate through the system. Reduced capacity can lead to tighter constraints, limiting the system's ability to absorb variability. Flexibility decreases as resources become more limited, increasing sensitivity to subsequent disturbances. Fragility increases because the system operates closer to its thresholds. These secondary effects are not direct consequences of the initial loss but emerge from the altered configuration that the loss creates.

The incorrect interpretation isolates loss as a single event with bounded impact. It assumes that once the immediate effect of the loss is accounted for, the system can resume normal operation. This ignores the propagation of loss through system dynamics. The reduced base affects not only future gains but also the system's ability to manage risk, allocate resources, and maintain stability. Loss therefore has a cascading effect, influencing multiple components over time.

Over multiple cycles, compounding disruption leads to divergence between systems that experience losses and those that do not. Even if subsequent performance is identical, the system that experienced loss accumulates less over time because it operates from a reduced base. This divergence increases with each cycle, as the gap in absolute accumulation widens. The effect is cumulative and persistent, reinforcing the structural disadvantage introduced by loss.

The failure of symmetric recovery assumptions emerges from the interaction of these dynamics. Systems that assume losses and gains offset linearly miscalculate the recovery required to restore prior states. They evaluate performance based on average outcomes, treating gains and losses as equivalent contributions to a net result. This approach obscures the nonlinear relationship between loss magnitude and recovery requirements, leading to systematic underestimation of downside impact.

At a first level, this miscalculation appears as a discrepancy between expected and actual recovery. Systems anticipate returning to prior levels after a sequence of gains that mirror previous losses, but the reduced base prevents full recovery. The system appears to be performing adequately based on average metrics, yet it remains below its prior state. This gap persists because the recovery requirement was underestimated.

Mechanistically, symmetric assumptions lead to overexposure. By underestimating the impact of loss, systems allocate more capacity to positions or structures that can generate gains but also carry downside risk. The expectation that losses can be offset by subsequent gains reduces the perceived cost of downside exposure. This leads to configurations where the system is vulnerable to large drawdowns, because the asymmetry of recovery is not accounted for in the initial allocation.

The incorrect interpretation reinforces itself across cycles. When losses do not immediately result in system failure, the assumption of recoverability is validated. The system continues to operate under the belief that gains will compensate for losses, increasing exposure over time. When a sufficiently large loss occurs, the recovery requirement exceeds expectations, and the system confronts the structural limits imposed by asymmetry.

This produces structural fragility. The system becomes dependent on favorable sequences of gains to maintain stability, because it has not constrained the magnitude of potential losses. Stability is therefore contingent rather than structural. It persists only as long as losses remain within recoverable bounds, which are often underestimated due to symmetric assumptions.

The structural implication is that downside governs system stability. Because losses impose nonlinear recovery requirements, compress time, and disrupt compounding, their impact on the system exceeds that of equivalent gains. Preventing or limiting loss preserves the base from which the system operates, maintaining its capacity to generate future gains and absorb variability. Gains contribute to accumulation, but they do not restore lost capacity on equal terms once a significant decline has occurred.

At a first level, this establishes a hierarchy between loss and gain. Loss has priority because it defines the boundaries within which the system can function. Gains operate within these boundaries, expanding the system's position but not altering the fundamental constraints imposed by loss asymmetry. The system's stability is therefore determined by its ability to avoid or contain losses that would push it beyond recoverable thresholds.

Mechanistically, limiting downside preserves compounding continuity. By maintaining the base, the system ensures that future gains can build on an intact foundation. This continuity allows accumulation to proceed without interruption, avoiding the drag introduced by recovery processes. The system remains within a regime where growth is additive rather than restorative, reducing the time and effort required to achieve progression.

The incorrect interpretation treats upside maximization as the primary driver of stability. It assumes that increasing gains will compensate for losses and improve overall system performance. This overlooks the asymmetry in recovery requirements and the disruption caused by loss. As a result, systems that prioritize gain without constraining loss may experience periods of rapid growth followed by significant drawdowns that negate prior gains and introduce long recovery periods.

Across multiple cycles, the dominance of downside becomes more pronounced. Systems that avoid large losses maintain a consistent accumulation path, while systems that experience drawdowns exhibit volatility in their trajectory. The cumulative effect of avoided losses is greater than the cumulative effect of additional gains, because the preserved base allows compounding to operate uninterrupted.

Stability therefore depends on controlling loss magnitude relative to system capacity. The system must be evaluated based on its exposure to losses that exceed recoverable thresholds. This evaluation shifts focus from average performance to boundary conditions. It emphasizes the importance of maintaining a configuration where losses remain within limits that the system can absorb without entering prolonged recovery states.

This establishes loss asymmetry as a governing constraint across all system behavior. Every process that generates gain must be considered in relation to the potential for loss and the associated recovery requirements. The system's trajectory is shaped not by its ability to produce gains alone, but by its ability to maintain continuity in the presence of variability. Stability emerges from the capacity to absorb loss without structural failure, defining the limits within which all other dynamics operate.

The Latent Risk Mechanism

The Latent Risk Mechanism defines risk as a continuous condition embedded within system structure rather than as a phenomenon that emerges only when an event occurs. Risk is not created at the moment of disruption; it exists prior to disruption as a function of configuration. The system carries exposure at all times, regardless of whether that exposure is activated. Events do not generate risk; they reveal it. This distinction separates the existence of vulnerability from the observation of its consequences, establishing that risk persists in an unobserved state until conditions align for activation.

At a first level, this reframes risk from something episodic into something persistent. Instead of appearing at discrete intervals, risk remains present as a constant attribute of system design. It is embedded in how resources are arranged, how dependencies are structured, and how capacity is allocated relative to potential disturbance. The system does not alternate between states of risk and safety; it operates continuously under conditions of exposure. The presence or absence of events does not alter this condition.

Mechanistically, this continuity means that risk accumulates silently between observable disruptions. The system may appear stable because no triggering event has occurred, but the underlying exposure remains unchanged. The absence of activation does not indicate the absence of vulnerability. Instead, it indicates that the conditions required to activate that vulnerability have not yet been met. Risk therefore operates independently of observation. It exists whether or not it is being expressed.

The incorrect interpretation treats risk as event-triggered. Under this model, risk is perceived to increase when disruptions occur and decrease when they do not. This creates a reactive framework in which the system evaluates its condition based on recent events. Periods without disruption are interpreted as periods of low risk, while periods with disruption are interpreted as periods of high risk. This interpretation collapses the distinction between exposure and activation, leading the system to misread its own structural state.

Latent exposure represents the embedded presence of vulnerability within system configuration. It is the portion of the system that would be affected if certain conditions were to occur, regardless of whether those conditions are currently active. Exposure is not contingent on events; it is defined by how the system is arranged. Dependencies, concentrations, and capacity limits all contribute to latent exposure. These elements exist continuously, shaping the system's potential response to disturbance.

At a first level, latent exposure can be understood as the system's readiness to be affected. It defines the pathways through which disruption would propagate if triggered. These pathways are not created at the moment of disruption; they are preconfigured within the system. The event merely activates them. The magnitude of impact is therefore determined before the event occurs, embedded in the system's structure.

Mechanistically, latent exposure behaves as a dormant state with conditional activation. It remains inactive until specific conditions are met, but its presence influences system behavior even in inactivity. The system's capacity, flexibility, and tolerance are all shaped by the level of exposure it carries. High exposure reduces the margin for error, even if no disruption is currently occurring. This creates a persistent constraint on system operation, limiting how much variability can be absorbed without triggering instability.

The incorrect interpretation assumes that exposure becomes relevant only when events occur. Under this assumption, systems do not account for latent conditions in their evaluation. They focus on observed disturbances rather than on embedded vulnerabilities. This leads to configurations where exposure is allowed to increase without immediate consequence, because its effects are not visible in the absence of activation. The system therefore accumulates vulnerability while appearing stable.

Across multiple cycles, latent exposure tends to expand when it is not actively constrained. In periods without disruption, the absence of visible consequences is interpreted as validation of the current configuration. This validation encourages further expansion of the same structural patterns that created the exposure. Dependencies deepen, concentrations increase, and margins narrow. Because no immediate feedback is generated, the system interprets this expansion as safe. The exposure grows silently, increasing the potential magnitude of future disruption.

A second layer of this mechanism emerges when considering system lock-in. As exposure accumulates, the system becomes more dependent on the conditions that have allowed it to remain unactivated. Stability becomes contingent on the continuation of those conditions. The system's configuration adapts to the absence of disruption, embedding assumptions about continuity that may not hold. When conditions change, the accumulated exposure is activated across a larger portion of the system, producing a more severe outcome than earlier configurations would have generated.

Apparent stability can mask underlying fragility because stability reflects the absence of disruption, not the absence of risk. A system can exhibit consistent performance, predictable outcomes, and low variability while carrying significant latent exposure. The observable behavior of the system does not reveal its underlying vulnerability. Stability, in this context, is an output of current conditions, not a measure of structural resilience.

At a first level, this masking effect occurs because the system is evaluated based on observed outcomes. When outcomes are stable, the system is assumed to be robust. However, this assumption conflates performance with structure. Performance reflects how the system behaves under current conditions, while structure determines how the system will behave when conditions change. A system can perform well while being structurally fragile if it is operating within a narrow range of conditions that do not activate its vulnerabilities.

Mechanistically, stability masking operates through the absence of feedback. Fragility does not produce signals until it is activated. As long as the system remains within conditions that do not trigger its vulnerabilities, there is no indication of their presence. This creates an information gap. The system lacks visibility into its own exposure because the conditions required to reveal that exposure have not occurred. As a result, stability is interpreted as evidence of strength rather than as a condition that may be concealing weakness.

The incorrect interpretation equates stability with safety. It assumes that consistent outcomes indicate low risk. This leads to an evaluation framework where variability is treated as risk and consistency is treated as security. Under this framework, systems that exhibit stable performance are considered robust, even if they carry significant latent exposure. This misinterpretation reinforces configurations that prioritize short-term stability over structural resilience.

Over time, the masking effect intensifies as stability persists. Each additional period without disruption reinforces the perception that the system is secure. This perception reduces the perceived need to examine underlying structure, allowing exposure to remain unaddressed. The system becomes increasingly confident in its stability, even as its fragility increases. This divergence between perception and reality creates a condition where the system is least prepared at the point where risk is highest.

A second expansion of this mechanism reveals a feedback loop between stability and fragility. As stability persists, the system optimizes for the conditions that produce it. This optimization often involves increasing efficiency, reducing redundancy, and concentrating resources. These changes improve performance under stable conditions but increase exposure to disruption. The system becomes more fragile as it becomes more stable, creating a paradox where the appearance of strength coincides with the growth of vulnerability.

Time without disruption does not indicate reduced risk because risk is not depleted through inactivity. The passage of time does not remove latent exposure; it merely delays its activation. Unlike observable variables that decay or dissipate, structural exposure remains embedded until it is actively altered. Time therefore has no mitigating effect on risk unless it is accompanied by changes in configuration.

At a first level, this can be understood as persistence of condition. The system's vulnerabilities do not weaken simply because they have not been activated. If anything, the lack of activation can allow them to persist unchallenged. The system does not become safer over time in the absence of disruption; it becomes older within the same structural constraints. The underlying exposure remains constant unless the system actively changes its configuration.

Mechanistically, time can increase the potential impact of risk rather than reduce it. As the system continues to operate, it may accumulate additional dependencies, expand its scale, or deepen its commitments. These changes increase exposure without altering the probability of triggering events. The system therefore becomes more vulnerable over time, even though it experiences no disruption. Time acts as an amplifier of exposure when it is coupled with structural expansion.

The incorrect interpretation treats time as a stabilizing factor. It assumes that if disruption has not occurred over a given period, the likelihood of disruption decreases or the system's resilience increases.

This assumption confuses absence of evidence with evidence of absence. It leads to the belief that risk diminishes with time, encouraging the system to maintain or expand its current configuration without addressing underlying vulnerabilities.

Across multiple cycles, this misinterpretation creates a cumulative effect. Each period without disruption reinforces the belief that the system is safe, reducing attention to latent exposure. The system becomes increasingly reliant on the continuation of stable conditions, embedding this assumption into its structure. When disruption eventually occurs, it does so against a backdrop of elevated exposure and reduced preparedness, amplifying its impact.

The accumulation of invisible risk occurs as latent exposure builds within system configuration without producing observable signals. Risk does not accumulate through events; it accumulates through structural changes that increase vulnerability. These changes can occur gradually, often as a byproduct of normal system operation. As the system evolves, it may increase its scale, concentrate its dependencies, or reduce its margins, each of which contributes to greater exposure.

At a first level, invisible accumulation is characterized by the absence of immediate feedback. The system does not register the increase in risk because no disruption occurs. The changes that increase exposure are not perceived as risky because their effects are not immediately visible. This creates a condition where risk grows silently, embedded in the system's structure.

Mechanistically, accumulation operates through compounding exposure. Each structural change adds to the system's vulnerability, and these additions interact. Dependencies that were previously isolated may become interconnected, increasing the pathways through which disruption can propagate. Margins that were previously sufficient may become constrained as commitments expand. The system's capacity to absorb disturbance decreases incrementally, even as its performance appears stable.

The incorrect interpretation focuses on event frequency rather than structural change. It assumes that risk is static in the absence of events, leading to a failure to account for the gradual increase in exposure. This results in a disconnect between the system's perceived risk and its actual vulnerability. The system believes it is operating under constant risk conditions, while in reality, its exposure is increasing.

Over time, invisible accumulation leads to threshold formation. The system approaches points where small disturbances can produce disproportionate effects because the accumulated exposure has reduced its tolerance. These thresholds are not visible through observation of events; they are embedded in the system's structure. When a disturbance occurs, the system crosses these thresholds, revealing the accumulated risk in a sudden and often severe manner.

A second expansion of this mechanism highlights lock-in effects. As exposure accumulates, the system becomes constrained in its ability to reverse the changes that created it. Dependencies become entrenched, commitments become fixed, and flexibility decreases. The system cannot easily reduce its exposure without incurring significant cost or disruption. This lock-in reinforces the accumulation of risk, as the system continues to operate within a configuration that it cannot easily alter.

The misinterpretation of calm periods emerges as a direct consequence of these dynamics. Calm periods are intervals in which no visible disruption occurs. They are often interpreted as evidence that the system is safe, stable, or well-configured. This interpretation arises from the event-based model of risk, where the absence of events is equated with the absence of risk. However, calm periods provide no information about latent exposure. They indicate only that activation has not occurred.

At a first level, this misinterpretation shifts the system's evaluation criteria. Instead of assessing structure, the system assesses outcomes.

Calm periods are treated as positive feedback, reinforcing existing configurations. The system becomes more confident in its stability, reducing scrutiny of underlying vulnerabilities. This confidence is not based on structural improvement but on the absence of observed disruption.

Mechanistically, calm periods create a feedback loop that reinforces exposure. As the system interprets calm as safety, it continues to expand within the same structural patterns that generated latent risk. Exposure increases while perceived risk decreases. This divergence grows over time, creating a widening gap between the system's actual vulnerability and its perceived stability.

Across multiple cycles, this misinterpretation compounds. Each calm period strengthens the system's belief in its safety, leading to further expansion of exposure. The system becomes increasingly dependent on the continuation of calm conditions. When disruption eventually occurs, it is interpreted as an anomaly rather than as the activation of accumulated risk. This delays recognition of the underlying cause, prolonging the system's exposure to instability.

A second expansion reveals that calm periods contribute to system lock-in. As the system operates without disruption, it optimizes for the conditions that produce calm. This optimization often involves reducing redundancy, increasing efficiency, and concentrating resources. These changes improve performance under stable conditions but increase vulnerability to disruption. The system becomes structurally aligned with calm conditions, making it less adaptable when conditions change.

The failure surface emerges when latent exposure, accumulated over time and masked by stability, is activated by a triggering condition. The event itself is not the source of risk; it is the point at which the underlying exposure becomes visible. When thresholds are crossed, the system experiences a transition from apparent stability to observable instability. This transition is often abrupt because the accumulated risk is realized in a compressed interval.

This progression establishes that risk must be evaluated independent of event occurrence. The presence or absence of disruption provides incomplete information about the system's condition. Evaluation must focus on structure, not on observed events. Latent exposure, accumulation, and masking dynamics all operate continuously, shaping the system's vulnerability regardless of whether they are currently visible. The system's stability is therefore determined by its configuration under potential conditions, not by its performance under current conditions.

The Income Fragility Mechanism

The Income Fragility Mechanism defines how system stability is conditioned by the structure of income as a dependency channel. Income is not simply an inflow; it is the primary conduit through which capacity is replenished and obligations are sustained. The system does not operate independently of income; it is continuously coupled to it. This coupling establishes income as a foundational dependency channel, where continuity of inflow directly determines whether the system can maintain its structural integrity over time.

At a first level, income functions as the input layer that supports all downstream activity. Obligations, resource allocation, and operational continuity are all contingent on the persistence of this input. When income flows consistently, the system maintains balance between demand and capacity. When income is disrupted, this balance is immediately affected because there is no independent mechanism that replaces its function. Income is therefore not one variable among many; it is the primary sustaining channel that anchors system operation.

Mechanistically, this dependency introduces continuous exposure. Because the system relies on income at each interval, it is perpetually sensitive to changes in that flow. Stability is not determined by total income over time but by the alignment between inflow timing and system demands. Even if aggregate income is sufficient, instability can emerge if the flow is disrupted at critical intervals. This makes income dependency time-sensitive as well as magnitude-dependent. The system must receive income when it is required, not merely in total.

The incorrect interpretation treats income as a static quantity rather than as a dynamic channel. Under this view, stability is assessed based on total or average income, ignoring how that income is delivered. This obscures the dependency structure. The system appears stable as long as aggregate income meets or exceeds obligations, even if the timing, continuity, or structure of that income introduces vulnerability. By focusing on totals rather than flow characteristics, the system underestimates its reliance on uninterrupted income.

Across multiple cycles, the dependency on income becomes self-reinforcing. As stable income persists, the system aligns more of its structure around that continuity. Obligations are calibrated to expected inflow, and capacity is allocated under the assumption that income will continue without interruption. This creates a reinforcing loop: stability leads to increased dependency, which in turn increases the system's sensitivity to disruption. The system becomes more stable under continuous income and more fragile in its absence.

A second expansion of this mechanism reveals lock-in effects. As the system adapts to stable income, it reduces flexibility. Buffers may be minimized, variability tolerance may narrow, and commitments may become fixed. These changes increase efficiency under stable conditions but reduce the system's ability to operate without income. The dependency on the income channel becomes structurally embedded, making it difficult to decouple without significant disruption.

Concentration risk emerges when the system relies on a limited number of income sources to sustain this dependency channel. Concentration is defined not by the presence of income but by the distribution of its sources. A system that derives income from a single source or a narrow set of sources concentrates its dependency, increasing the impact of any disruption to those sources. The fragility arises not from the level of income but from its structural distribution.

At a first level, concentration risk can be understood as a lack of diversification in the income channel. When income is concentrated, the system's entire capacity is tied to the continuity of a single pathway. If that pathway is disrupted, the system experiences a full loss of inflow rather than a partial reduction. This creates a binary condition where income is either present or absent, with limited intermediate states.

Mechanistically, concentration amplifies the effect of interruption. Because the system is dependent on a single source, any disruption to that source propagates across the entire system. There is no alternative pathway to absorb or offset the loss. The system transitions from full operation to constrained operation immediately, without a buffering effect from other sources. This creates a sharp discontinuity in capacity.

The incorrect interpretation assumes that concentration is acceptable as long as the source is stable. Under this assumption, the reliability of the source is treated as sufficient protection against risk. However, this ignores the structural impact of dependency. Even highly stable sources carry the potential for disruption. When disruption occurs, the concentrated structure amplifies its effect. Stability of the source does not eliminate fragility; it merely delays its activation.

Across multiple cycles, concentration tends to increase when income remains stable. As the system experiences consistent inflow from a limited number of sources, it reinforces its reliance on those sources. Additional income pathways may not be developed because the existing structure appears sufficient. This leads to increasing concentration over time, embedding fragility within the system.

A second expansion reveals that concentration creates path dependency. The system's configuration becomes aligned with the characteristics of the dominant income source. Timing, magnitude, and predictability of income shape how obligations and capacity are structured. This alignment reduces the system's ability to adapt to alternative income structures. When disruption occurs, the system cannot easily reconfigure, because its structure is optimized for a specific source that is no longer available.

Volatility and predictability represent distinct structural properties of income streams that influence fragility in different ways. Volatility refers to the variability of income magnitude over time. Predictability refers to the reliability of timing and occurrence. These properties are often conflated, but they operate independently. An income stream can be volatile but predictable in its timing, or stable in magnitude but unpredictable in its occurrence.

At a first level, volatility affects the system's ability to manage fluctuations in capacity. High volatility introduces variability in available resources, requiring the system to absorb changes in magnitude. Predictability affects the system's ability to align inflow with obligations. Even a stable income magnitude can create instability if it arrives unpredictably relative to demand.

Mechanistically, volatility and predictability interact with the system's dependency structure. High volatility requires capacity buffers to absorb variation, while low predictability requires timing flexibility to manage uncertainty. When income lacks predictability, the system cannot reliably match inflow to outflow, increasing the likelihood of timing mismatches. When income is volatile, the system must accommodate fluctuations in magnitude, which can strain capacity during low periods.

The incorrect interpretation treats volatility as the primary risk characteristic while overlooking predictability. Systems may focus on stabilizing income magnitude while ignoring the importance of consistent timing. This leads to configurations where income appears stable on average but introduces instability through irregular delivery. The system becomes vulnerable not because income is insufficient, but because it is misaligned with obligations.

Over multiple cycles, the interaction between volatility and predictability shapes system behavior. Systems with predictable but volatile income may develop mechanisms to absorb magnitude fluctuations, while systems with unpredictable income face persistent timing challenges. These differences influence how fragility manifests, even when total income levels are similar.

Structural instability differs from temporary fluctuation in that it reflects persistent characteristics of the income system rather than short-term deviations. Temporary fluctuation represents variations that occur within the system's capacity to absorb them. Structural instability arises when the characteristics of income exceed the system's tolerance, creating ongoing misalignment between inflow and demand.

At a first level, temporary fluctuations are bounded. The system can absorb them without altering its configuration. Structural instability, by contrast, produces recurring strain. The system cannot return to equilibrium because the underlying income characteristics consistently disrupt balance. This distinction is critical because it separates noise from structural weakness.

Mechanistically, structural instability emerges when volatility, unpredictability, or concentration exceed the system's capacity to manage them. The system experiences repeated periods of constraint, even if no single event is severe. These constraints accumulate, reducing flexibility and increasing sensitivity to disruption. The system operates in a state of continuous adjustment, indicating that the instability is embedded in its structure.

The incorrect interpretation treats all variation as temporary. Under this view, fluctuations are expected to resolve over time, leading the system to maintain its configuration despite persistent instability. This delays recognition of structural issues, allowing fragility to persist and potentially worsen.

Income interruption pathways define how disruptions in income propagate through the system. An interruption is not confined to the loss of inflow; it triggers a sequence of effects that extend across all dependent components. Because income is the primary dependency channel, its interruption affects every element that relies on it.

At a first level, interruption reduces available capacity. Obligations that were previously supported by income must now be met through alternative means or deferred. This creates immediate pressure on the system, as the balance between inflow and demand is disrupted. The system must adjust to a new capacity level, often under constrained conditions.

Mechanistically, interruption propagates through dependency chains. Fixed obligations continue regardless of income, creating a mismatch between demand and capacity. Variable components may adjust, but only within limits. As the interruption persists, the system exhausts its ability to absorb the deficit, leading to cascading effects. Each component that depends on income transmits the disruption to the next, amplifying its impact.

The incorrect interpretation isolates interruption as a discrete event. It assumes that the impact is limited to the duration of the interruption. This overlooks the propagation of effects through the system. Even after income resumes, the system may remain in a degraded state due to accumulated deficits or structural adjustments made during the interruption.

Across multiple cycles, interruption pathways reveal how fragility is distributed. Systems with concentrated dependency experience immediate and widespread disruption, while systems with distributed dependency may experience partial effects. The structure of dependency determines how interruption translates into system-wide impact.

A second expansion highlights failure conditions. When interruption coincides with high dependency and limited flexibility, the system crosses thresholds where obligations cannot be sustained. Failure emerges not from the interruption itself but from the system's inability to absorb it. The interruption acts as a trigger that reveals the underlying fragility created by dependency concentration.

Dependency amplification occurs when fixed obligations increase the system's reliance on continuous income. Fixed obligations represent commitments that must be met regardless of income variability. They create a baseline demand that the system must satisfy at each interval. As fixed obligations increase, the system's dependency on income becomes more rigid.

At a first level, fixed obligations reduce flexibility. The system cannot easily adjust its demand in response to changes in income. This creates a condition where even small disruptions in income can produce disproportionate effects, because the system has limited ability to reduce its requirements.

Mechanistically, fixed obligations amplify the impact of interruption. When income is disrupted, the system must continue to meet these obligations, increasing the strain on remaining capacity. This accelerates the propagation of disruption, as the system has fewer options to absorb the deficit. The presence of fixed obligations therefore increases the sensitivity of the system to income changes.

The incorrect interpretation treats obligations as independent of income structure. It assumes that as long as income is sufficient under normal conditions, obligations can be sustained. This ignores the interaction between obligations and income variability. Fixed obligations create rigidity that increases fragility when income is not continuous.

Across multiple cycles, dependency amplification leads to increased fragility. As obligations become fixed and persistent, the system's ability to adapt decreases. Stability becomes contingent on uninterrupted income, and any deviation introduces immediate strain. The system becomes increasingly sensitive to changes in its primary dependency channel.

A second expansion reveals lock-in effects similar to those observed in concentration. Fixed obligations anchor the system to a specific income level and structure. Reducing these obligations often requires structural change, which may not be feasible without disruption. This lock-in reinforces dependency, making the system more vulnerable to income interruption.

The progression of these mechanisms establishes that fragility originates from dependency concentration. Income serves as the primary channel through which capacity is sustained, and when this channel is concentrated, volatile, or rigidly coupled to obligations, the system becomes structurally vulnerable. The magnitude of income is secondary to its configuration. Fragility is not defined by how much income the system receives, but by how dependent it is on specific income structures and how that dependency interacts with obligations and variability.

The Expense Shock Mechanism

The Expense Shock Mechanism describes how systems experience instability through the structure, sequencing, and concentration of expense demands rather than through expense presence alone. Expenses are often treated as stable because many of them recur and can be named in advance, but recurrence does not eliminate variability. The appearance of stability comes from familiarity, not from structural uniformity. Even where baseline obligations remain recognizable from cycle to cycle, the total expense load imposed on the system is never perfectly fixed. Expense behavior is inherently variable because timing shifts, magnitudes change, related demands converge, and irregular costs emerge inside what appears, from a distance, to be a repeating pattern. The mechanism begins by separating perceived stability from actual expense behavior. A system may believe its costs are stable because its categories remain stable, while the operational burden created by those categories remains variable in timing, density, and size.

At a first level, expense variability means that outflows do not arrive as a smooth or evenly distributed stream. They arrive as demands attached to dates, intervals, and conditions. Some recur monthly, some quarterly, some seasonally, and some only when triggered by replacement, maintenance, lapse, or external change. Even where the nominal structure seems familiar, the actual burden placed on the system changes as these demands interact. Stability of label does not imply stability of load. Rent can be known, insurance can be known, utilities can be expected, and maintenance can be anticipated in category form, yet the actual distribution of outflow across time can still remain uneven. The system therefore confronts variability not because expenses are random in every instance, but because the burden they create is structurally non-uniform.

At a deeper level, perceived stability itself becomes a distortion. Because many expense categories recur, the system interprets repetition as predictability and predictability as smoothness. This is incorrect. Predictability of category differs from predictability of total load at each operating interval. A recurring expense system can remain highly variable if the expenses concentrate at particular points, fluctuate in size, or interact with one another in ways that compress pressure into narrow windows. What appears stable at the annual level may be unstable at the weekly or monthly level. This matters because systems fail at intervals, not at abstract annual averages. The system must absorb actual expense density when it arrives, not a theoretical average distributed across the full period.

The incorrect interpretation treats expenses as stable because they are familiar. Under that view, the existence of known recurring costs is taken as evidence that the system is operating in a controlled environment. This flattens the distinction between recognizability and structural manageability. A system can recognize its expense categories and still remain highly sensitive to the way those expenses arrive. Familiarity lowers perceived uncertainty, but it does not reduce actual concentration, rigidity, or timing pressure. As a result, the system may underestimate how much variation exists inside what looks like a normal expense pattern.

Across repeated cycles, this misreading produces cumulative vulnerability. Each period that appears manageable reinforces the belief that the expense structure is stable, even when the system is repeatedly absorbing uneven pressure. Instead of identifying variability as structural, the system treats stressed intervals as isolated inconveniences. The recurring pattern of uneven load is normalized rather than evaluated. This delays recognition that expense instability is embedded in the structure itself. Over time, a system can become highly practiced at surviving variable expenses without ever correctly identifying that variability is the governing condition.

Expense events do not distribute evenly over time. They cluster. This clustering is central to the mechanism because system stress is generated less by total expense volume than by concentrated outflow density within limited intervals. A system can absorb a given amount of expense when it is dispersed, and fail under the same total amount when it is compressed. Expense clustering means that multiple outflows arrive in temporal proximity, forcing the system to meet several demands before it has had sufficient time to recover from the prior ones. The burden is therefore not additive in a simple sense. It is compressive. It narrows the interval in which adjustment is possible.

At a first level, clustering can be understood as the convergence of expense demands within the same operating window. Fixed bills may align with periodic obligations, maintenance may emerge alongside routine payments, and irregular costs may arrive during already dense expense intervals. The result is not merely a larger total; it is a more difficult burden because the system must absorb multiple outflows before replenishment, redistribution, or recovery can occur. Expense stress therefore depends on sequencing, not only on amount.

At a deeper level, clustering changes the geometry of pressure. When expenses are dispersed, the system has time between outflows to replenish capacity, reallocate liquidity, or allow income inflows to arrive. When they cluster, those adjustment windows disappear. The system experiences the expenses as a combined load rather than as separate items. This combined load can push the system beyond tolerance even if none of the individual expenses would have done so alone. Clustering therefore converts individually manageable demands into structurally destabilizing episodes through compression of time.

The incorrect interpretation treats expense events as independent. Under that model, each cost is evaluated on its own terms. If no single expense appears excessive, the system assumes the total burden is manageable. This ignores the fact that expenses are absorbed in sequence, not in isolation. Several moderate demands arriving together can produce more stress than one large demand arriving alone. The system's tolerance is interval-based, so clustering matters more than isolated magnitude analysis suggests.

Across multiple cycles, clustering can become a repeating structural pattern rather than an occasional anomaly. Certain periods may reliably carry dense outflow concentration due to billing schedules, seasonal demands, renewal structures, or deferred maintenance cycles. If the system interprets these intervals as exceptional each time they occur, it fails to identify clustering as a built-in feature of the expense structure. Repeated clustered periods then reinforce sensitivity. The system does not merely experience occasional pressure; it repeatedly enters compressed states in which flexibility narrows and tolerance is tested. This repeated pattern can normalize instability without resolving it.

A second layer of this mechanism reveals that clustering interacts with other structural properties to magnify pressure downstream. Once expenses begin to converge, the significance of fixed commitments, income timing, and available flexibility increases sharply. Clustering exposes weaknesses that remain partly hidden under dispersed expense conditions. A system may appear workable under ordinary spacing, yet become unstable when those same obligations are forced into tighter intervals. Clustering therefore acts as a revealing condition. It does not create fragility from nothing; it exposes sensitivity already embedded in the structure.

The distinction between fixed and flexible cost structures defines how a system responds when expense pressure rises. Fixed costs are demands that persist with limited short-term adjustability. They continue across intervals regardless of temporary pressure, and their amount or timing is often difficult to alter without structural change. Flexible costs, by contrast, are expenses whose timing, magnitude, or occurrence can adjust more readily in response to changing system conditions. This distinction is not a moral or behavioral one. It is a property of system design. It determines how much of the expense base remains rigid when pressure enters the system.

At a first level, fixed costs create a baseline operating load that the system must carry continuously. They establish the minimum outflow requirement necessary to maintain current structure. Flexible costs sit above or around this baseline, allowing some degree of variation in how demand is expressed. The balance between the two determines whether the system can adapt when expense shocks occur. A system with a high fixed-cost share enters each interval already committed to substantial outflow. A system with more flexible cost structure retains greater room to absorb disturbance without immediate structural stress.

At a deeper level, fixed and flexible cost structures shape not just immediate response capacity, but the overall behavior of the system under repeated pressure. Fixed cost systems are stable under uninterrupted support conditions because they regularize much of the expense base. However, that regularity creates rigidity. When conditions change, the system cannot easily reduce demand. Flexible cost systems may exhibit more day-to-day variation, but they possess more adaptive capacity because outflows can be delayed, reduced, or redistributed with less structural friction. The relevant distinction is therefore not neatness versus disorder, but rigidity versus elasticity under stress.

The incorrect interpretation treats fixed costs as inherently stabilizing because they are known in advance. Their predictability is mistaken for safety. Yet predictability of obligation does not reduce pressure if the obligation remains immovable when the system's capacity changes. A known demand can still be destabilizing if it remains due in full during periods of reduced tolerance. Conversely, flexible costs may appear less orderly because they vary, but their adjustability can reduce system sensitivity under shock conditions. The error lies in equating visibility with resilience.

Across multiple cycles, high fixed-cost structures create lock-in. Stable periods encourage the maintenance or expansion of rigid commitments because those commitments appear sustainable when income and liquidity remain aligned. Each cycle of successful payment reinforces the structure. Over time, a larger share of the system becomes committed in advance, narrowing the range of possible adjustment during future stress. The system becomes increasingly dependent on continuity, not because total expenses necessarily rise beyond all limits, but because the share of expenses that can move without damage declines.

A second expansion reveals that fixed-cost dominance changes the failure surface of the system. When pressure emerges, the system cannot spread the burden across the full expense base. It must absorb shock through the small portion that remains adjustable, or through liquidity depletion, deferral, or structural break. This means the effective pressure imposed by a shock is greater than its nominal size. The system is not choosing across all costs; it is reacting within a narrow band of flexibility. As fixed commitments rise, the same external disturbance produces increasingly concentrated internal stress. Rigidity therefore does not merely coexist with expense shock. It acts as a force multiplier.

Shock amplification through rigidity follows directly from this structure. An expense shock becomes destabilizing not only because of its size, but because it enters a system where much of the existing load cannot move. Rigidity amplifies shock by converting a discrete cost increase into broader system pressure. When a shock arrives, the system cannot distribute adjustment evenly. It must force the burden through constrained channels, which intensifies disruption. The more rigid the preexisting structure, the larger the secondary effects produced by the same initial event.

At a first level, amplification means that the shock exceeds its own nominal magnitude. A large repair, medical bill, lapse correction, or concentrated renewal does not only add its amount to the expense total. It also triggers rearrangement pressure across every rigidly committed element surrounding it. Because baseline obligations remain fixed, the shock must be absorbed by whatever remains: liquidity reserves, delayed payments, compressed discretionary space, or short-term financing substitutions. The result is that the shock imposes both direct cost and indirect system strain.

At a deeper level, rigidity changes the transmission path of shock. In a more adaptable structure, an unexpected expense can be distributed through timing adjustments, load reduction, or temporary reallocation. In a rigid structure, those channels are limited. The shock therefore travels more quickly from local disturbance to system-wide pressure. Liquidity buffers are drawn down faster. Timing gaps become harder to bridge. Additional obligations begin to compete rather than sequence. A shock that might have remained contained in an elastic system becomes propagative in a rigid one.

The incorrect interpretation treats shocks as isolated anomalies whose significance depends mainly on their size. This underestimates the role of structure. The same shock magnitude does not produce the same outcome across systems. Its effect depends on how much of the system is already immovable. When rigidity is high, moderate shocks can destabilize. When rigidity is lower, even large shocks may remain absorbable. The event is therefore not the explanatory center. The structure is.

Over repeated cycles, rigid systems develop reinforcement patterns that increase shock amplification. Successful navigation of prior shocks often does not reduce rigidity; it may preserve or even justify it. Because the system survived earlier disturbances, the underlying structure is treated as adequate. Yet each recovery may come at the cost of buffer depletion, increased compression, or reduced future flexibility. This means that the same level of rigidity can produce greater sensitivity over time even if nominal obligations do not rise. Past survival is mistaken for structural strength, while actual tolerance may be narrowing beneath the surface.

A second pass into this mechanism reveals failure emergence conditions. Rigidity becomes most dangerous when clustered expenses or income delays occur before the system has restored flexibility from prior stress. Under these conditions, the shock is not entering a neutral structure but a partially compressed one. The rigid cost base continues unchanged while recovery capacity remains incomplete. The system then crosses from pressure into instability not because the new shock is unprecedented, but because rigidity prevented restoration between cycles. Lock-in therefore matters here as well. Fixed commitments do not merely amplify a single shock; they preserve vulnerability across intervals.

Timing mismatch between income and expenses introduces another structural layer of sensitivity. Stability depends not only on whether income and expenses balance over a broad period, but on whether income arrives before or at the intervals when expenses must be paid. Timing mismatch occurs when inflows and outflows are misaligned across operating windows. Under mismatch conditions, the system can exhibit adequacy in aggregate and still enter acute pressure because the required capacity is absent at the moment the expense arrives. This makes timing a structural variable, not an administrative detail.

At a first level, mismatch appears when scheduled expenses concentrate before corresponding income inflows, or when irregular expenses arrive during low-liquidity windows. Even when expected income remains intact, the system may be unable to meet obligations without drawing down buffers or introducing temporary substitutions. The issue is not long-run insufficiency but interval misalignment. Because systems operate continuously rather than at end-of-period averages, timing gaps create real stress even where totals appear sustainable.

At a deeper level, timing mismatch functions as a conversion mechanism through which otherwise manageable expense structures become unstable. Fixed costs that are absorbable under synchronized inflow become burdensome under delayed inflow. Clustered expenses become more severe when they occur before replenishment. Large expenses become nonlinear when they arrive at the weakest point in the income cycle. Timing therefore links all prior sections. Expense variability, clustering, and rigidity all become more dangerous when they encounter inflow misalignment. Mismatch is not a separate problem layered on top of expense structure; it is the condition that determines when structural sensitivity becomes active.

The incorrect interpretation evaluates stability on net balance alone. If monthly income exceeds monthly expenses, the system is presumed stable. This compresses time out of analysis. It ignores the fact that obligations mature on dates, not at average monthly endpoints. A system with positive net surplus can still fail to meet obligations if the sequence of inflows and outflows is misaligned. The average view obscures interval stress, and interval stress is where instability emerges.

Across multiple cycles, repeated timing mismatches produce chronic sensitivity. The system begins each period with unresolved pressure from the prior one, forcing it to rely on rolling compensation mechanisms rather than genuine equilibrium. Liquidity reserves become timing bridges instead of protective buffers. Flexible expenses are deferred not because they disappeared, but because they were displaced into future intervals. This shifts rather than solves the problem. The repeated use of future capacity to resolve present mismatch creates cumulative compression across cycles, increasing fragility even if headline income and expense figures remain unchanged.

A second expansion shows how timing mismatch can lock systems into unstable operating rhythms. Once a structure begins depending on temporary bridging measures to resolve ordinary sequencing gaps, those measures become part of baseline functioning. The system no longer uses liquidity to absorb unusual stress; it uses it to survive normal timing. This lowers tolerance for genuine shocks because the margin has already been consumed by routine mismatch. Failure then emerges when an additional expense arrives before prior timing deficits have been repaired. Again, the destabilizing force is not the event alone. It is the structural dependence on precise sequencing in a system that lacks sufficient timing flexibility.

The impact of large expenses is non-linear because large or concentrated outflows do not simply increase pressure in proportion to their size. They alter the state of the system. A small increase in expense may create manageable tightening. A large expense can collapse adjustment space, accelerate liquidity depletion, force deferral of other obligations, and move the system across structural thresholds. This is why large expenses cannot be evaluated as scaled-up versions of ordinary ones. Their effect changes qualitatively as magnitude and concentration rise.

At a first level, non-linearity appears because tolerance is not infinite and not evenly distributed. A system may absorb modest shocks within ordinary variation, but once an expense exceeds available slack, the consequences expand rapidly. The expense then triggers secondary effects: other payments are displaced, timing gaps widen, and the remaining cost structure becomes harder to sustain. The relationship between expense size and system impact therefore steepens beyond certain points. Each additional unit of expense produces more than an additional unit of stress once thresholds are crossed.

At a deeper level, large expenses often arrive with concentration features that amplify their impact beyond magnitude alone. A major expense rarely enters an empty structure. It arrives into an existing field of recurring obligations, timing commitments, and partially used capacity.

Its effect therefore depends on what it collides with. If it lands during a dense expense window, inside a rigid cost structure, or before income replenishment, the disturbance is not simply large; it is state-changing. It converts a stable interval into a compressed one, or a compressed interval into a destabilized one. Non-linearity thus arises through interaction between size and structure.

The incorrect interpretation assumes that expense impact scales proportionally. Under that view, a large expense is just a bigger version of a small expense, so analysis focuses on whether the nominal amount fits inside some broad budget measure. This misses threshold behavior. The critical question is not only whether the system can mathematically account for the amount across time, but whether the amount pushes the system across boundaries where normal adjustment no longer functions. Once those boundaries are crossed, recovery requirements increase disproportionately because the system must repair not only the direct outflow but the secondary disruptions the expense created.

Across repeated cycles, large expenses can create persistent structural aftereffects. They reduce the base from which future expenses are absorbed, consume timing flexibility, and leave unresolved pressures that carry into subsequent intervals. Even after the discrete expense has passed, the system may remain in a weakened state because buffers are lower, deferrals have accumulated, and rigid obligations continue unchanged. A later moderate expense can then produce severe pressure because it enters a system already altered by prior concentration. This is how non-linear impact extends across time. The original event does not end when it is paid; its structural consequences remain embedded in the system's subsequent sensitivity.

A second pass into the non-linear mechanism reveals failure emergence more precisely. Failure occurs when a large or concentrated expense not only exceeds available slack but also disables the system's normal methods of adaptation. Once liquidity bridging, timing adjustment, or limited flexibility are exhausted, the system is no longer absorbing shock; it is breaching structure. Payments begin to compete in ways the system cannot resolve internally. Obligations become mutually incompatible within the available interval. At that point, the importance of expense size lies less in its absolute number than in its ability to force a transition from variance management to structural breakdown.

The progression of this mechanism establishes that expense structure determines system sensitivity. Variability hidden beneath perceived stability, clustering of demands, the ratio of fixed to flexible costs, rigidity-based amplification, mismatch between inflow and outflow timing, and the non-linear behavior of large expenses all point to the same underlying principle: systems are not destabilized by expenses merely because expenses exist, but because expenses are arranged in ways that determine how pressure is absorbed. Sensitivity is therefore structural. Two systems can face similar total expense levels and exhibit radically different stability outcomes because their expense structures differ in density, rigidity, sequencing, and concentration. The decisive variable is not cost presence alone, but the configuration through which cost moves across time and interacts with available capacity.

The Asset & Access Risk Mechanism

Ownership does not guarantee accessibility.

The Asset & Access Risk Mechanism defines a structural separation between possessing value and being able to deploy value when conditions require it. An asset can exist on a balance sheet, contribute to net worth, and represent substantial stored value while remaining unusable at the moment the system needs operational support. This mechanism begins by rejecting the assumption that ownership and access are equivalent. They are not. Ownership is a legal or economic claim on value. Accessibility is the system's ability to convert that claim into usable capacity within the interval in which pressure emerges. The distinction matters because systems do not survive on nominal possession. They survive on deployable liquidity.

At a first level, ownership indicates that value is held somewhere within the structure of the system. A property interest, account balance, security, private holding, or other asset may increase total resource representation. Yet this says nothing about whether the value can be used immediately, partially, or without disruption. Usability depends on the conditions attached to the asset: conversion time, transaction structure, market depth, withdrawal rules, legal restrictions, settlement timing, valuation uncertainty, and the presence or absence of counterparties. The system therefore cannot evaluate an asset only by asking whether it exists. It must also ask whether the asset can function as operative support under time pressure.

At a deeper level, this distinction exposes a common structural error. Systems often treat owned value as if it were available value. That compression removes friction from analysis. If all owned assets are counted as equally accessible, the system appears far more resilient than it actually is. It seems to possess broad fallback capacity because nominal value is mistaken for deployable reserve. In practice, assets exist across a hierarchy of access conditions. Some can be used immediately, some only after delay, some only at discount, and some only under conditions that may disappear precisely when access is most needed. Ownership therefore does not describe functional capacity. It describes stored claim. Functional capacity depends on the pathway between ownership and use.

The incorrect interpretation treats assets as interchangeable expressions of the same resource base. Under that view, value held in any form can be assumed to support stability because it exists somewhere within the system. This is analytically convenient but structurally false. Assets differ not only in value but in conversion behavior. A system that treats ownership as equivalent to usability effectively assumes away access risk. That produces inflated confidence during stable conditions and severe miscalculation when stress requires immediate deployment.

Across multiple cycles, this confusion reinforces itself. When stress does not occur, inaccessible assets are not tested. Because they remain untested, they continue to be counted as available support. Stable periods validate the assumption that ownership is sufficient, even though no actual conversion has been required. The system then expands commitments, reduces liquidity margins, or tolerates tighter structures because it believes its asset base provides protection. Over time, reliance on nominal ownership increases while actual access remains uncertain. The system becomes wealthier in representation and weaker in operable resilience.

A second layer of this mechanism reveals lock-in effects. As the system grows accustomed to treating asset ownership as fallback capacity, it may build its obligations and tolerance assumptions around resources that are not actually usable at decision speed. This creates a hidden dependency on future conversion under unknown conditions. If access later proves constrained, the system cannot simply replace that missing usability with the fact of ownership. The claim still exists, but the timing of use has failed. Structural fragility then emerges not because value was absent, but because accessibility was assumed rather than verified.

The distinction between ownership and usability follows directly from this separation. Ownership refers to possession or control of an asset as part of the system's resource structure. Usability refers to the capacity to mobilize that asset into action without excessive delay, loss, or conditional dependence. An owned asset may be valuable yet unusable within the interval that matters. This means the system can be resource-rich and operationally constrained at the same time. The contradiction is only apparent if ownership and usability are incorrectly treated as synonyms.

Usability is a timing-sensitive property. The relevant question is not whether an asset can be used eventually, but whether it can be used before system pressure crosses into instability. A resource that becomes available after obligations have matured, after losses have propagated, or after strategic options have narrowed does not function as present support. It remains part of longer-term value, but it does not preserve short-term survival. This temporal distinction is central. Systems do not fail because value disappears abstractly. They fail because usable value is unavailable when the interval of stress arrives.

Usability is also conditional. Conversion may require market participation, formal approval, settlement processes, liquidation procedures, tax consequences, documentation, or acceptance of price concessions. Each condition introduces friction between the held asset and the moment of deployment. The more conditions required, the less the asset behaves like immediate support. From a structural perspective, this means assets occupy different liquidity tiers even when their nominal values are large. What matters is not only what the asset is worth, but what must happen before the system can draw capacity from it.

The incorrect interpretation defines value by holding alone. It assumes that once an asset is owned, its usefulness is inherent. This ignores conditionality. It also ignores the fact that the system's need for resources often arises under pressure, when those conditions may tighten rather than relax. An asset that appears usable under calm conditions may become materially less usable under stress. The distinction between ownership and usability therefore widens precisely when the system most needs it to narrow.

Over time, systems that do not separate these concepts begin to substitute representation for function. Balance sheet strength is allowed to stand in for liquidity strength. Total asset value is used to justify lower cash reserves or tighter operational margins. The system's apparent resilience increases in nominal terms while its actual response capacity declines. The more this pattern repeats across stable cycles, the more difficult it becomes to identify the gap, because visible distress remains absent until a conversion test occurs.

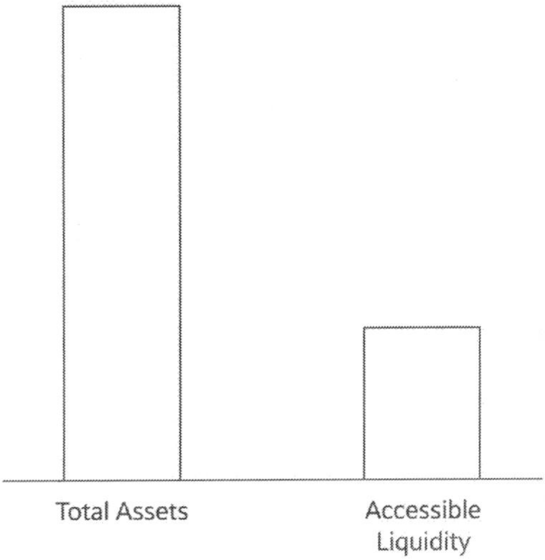

[Figure 3: Asset vs Accessible Liquidity Diagram]

Liquidity and valuation must also be separated. Valuation describes the estimated worth of an asset under given pricing assumptions. Liquidity describes the degree to which that asset can be converted into usable funds quickly, reliably, and without major value destruction. These are not adjacent versions of the same attribute. They are separate structural properties. An asset can carry high valuation and low liquidity. It can also carry modest valuation and high liquidity. Stability depends less on the abstract size of held value than on the proportion of that value that can become operational capacity without delay.

At a first level, valuation is a representational measure. It tells the system what an asset may be worth in a modeled or observed exchange environment. Liquidity is a functional measure. It tells the system how readily that value can be accessed and used. Valuation can remain high while liquidity deteriorates. This is because price and convertibility do not move together by necessity. A system may own a highly valued asset that cannot be sold quickly, borrowed against immediately, or accessed in usable increments. Conversely, an immediately available cash balance may have low nominal size but high stabilizing power because it is already in deployable form.

At a deeper level, valuation often creates a misleading sense of protection because it is legible, reportable, and numerically impressive. It expands the visible resource base and encourages the belief that the system is well-supported. Liquidity is less visually dramatic, because it is often smaller and narrower. Yet in operational terms, liquidity determines whether the system can absorb timing gaps, meet obligations, and preserve decision space. The asset's quoted or appraised value may matter in longer horizons. In short intervals of stress, liquidity governs. This produces a persistent structural tension between apparent wealth and usable resilience.

The incorrect interpretation assumes that high valuation can compensate for low liquidity. Under this assumption, resource sufficiency is judged by total asset value, with conversion presumed available when needed. This creates systematic overconfidence. The system behaves as though future liquidation or borrowing can always translate valuation into support. But valuation is contingent and abstract until realized. Liquidity is concrete and immediate. Treating them as interchangeable causes the system to rely on value that may not be mobilizable within the necessary timeframe.

Across multiple cycles, rising valuation can intensify this distortion. When asset prices increase or appraised values grow, the system experiences a visible expansion of worth. This may encourage tighter liquidity holdings because the larger balance sheet appears to provide ample fallback. Yet if the added value remains locked in illiquid form, the system has improved its valuation profile without improving its operational survivability. A widening divergence then develops between nominal strength and actual access. Stable or rising valuations mask the fact that liquidity may be unchanged or even declining relative to obligations.

A second expansion reveals a reinforcement pattern. When valuation growth occurs during calm periods, the absence of immediate access problems is interpreted as evidence that the asset structure is sufficient. Systems become more comfortable holding larger shares of value in slow-conversion forms. This creates dependency on unrealized worth. If stress later requires conversion, the system discovers that valuation did not eliminate access friction; it only concealed it during the period when conversion was unnecessary. Failure then emerges not from mispricing alone, but from using valuation as a substitute for liquidity in structural analysis.

Access constraints emerge most clearly under stress conditions. During calm periods, many assets appear convertible because markets function normally, counterparties are available, administrative processes are manageable, and time pressure is limited. Under stress, those conditions change. Access may narrow because the system itself is under pressure, because the surrounding environment becomes less accommodating, or because both occur simultaneously. The constraint is therefore not merely an asset characteristic in isolation. It is the interaction between the asset and the conditions of need.

At a first level, stress alters the practical route from value to usability. Approval thresholds may tighten, buyers may retreat, transaction times may extend, and partial liquidation may become difficult. Even where formal ownership is undisputed, actual deployment becomes constrained. The system experiences this not as a question of whether value exists, but whether that value can be reached in time, at scale, and without destabilizing concessions. The answer often deteriorates under stress, which means accessibility is state-dependent.

At a deeper level, this state dependence produces asymmetry between planning conditions and failure conditions. Assets are often evaluated when the system is calm, but they are needed when the system is strained. The conversion assumptions built in stable conditions are then carried into stressed conditions where they no longer hold. This is a structural error because it assumes access quality remains constant across states. In reality, stress frequently reduces both speed and reliability of access. The resource that looked available in theory becomes conditional in practice precisely when the system cannot tolerate conditionality.

The incorrect interpretation assumes that if an asset can be accessed in ordinary circumstances, it can be accessed in stressed ones. This ignores regime change. Stress is not merely ordinary operation with more urgency added. It alters counterpart behavior, internal tolerance, market depth, and acceptable transaction terms. The system that relies on ordinary-state accessibility during stress therefore overstates its fallback capacity.

Across repeated cycles, stress-based access constraints create a pattern of delayed recognition. Because most cycles do not test the full pathway from asset to usable liquidity, the system keeps counting constrained resources as if they were freely available. Only when a stress event occurs does the access assumption get tested. If the test fails, the discovery happens late, after other options have narrowed. The system then realizes that its resource base was partly illusory in operational terms. This late recognition is part of the mechanism. Access risk remains latent until stress converts it from abstraction into immediate limitation.

A second pass into this mechanism shows how systems adapt in the wrong direction. If prior calm periods allowed assets to appear dependable without actual conversion, the system may further concentrate value in access-constrained forms. This creates lock-in. More of the balance sheet becomes dependent on stable-state conditions for realizability. When stress arrives, not only is access reduced, but the system's structure is now more exposed to that reduction than before. Failure surfaces emerge when obligations require immediate liquidity while the asset base is trapped behind conditional conversion pathways.

Timing friction in asset conversion adds another layer. Even when an asset can eventually be accessed, the time required to convert it into usable liquidity may exceed the system's tolerance window. Timing friction refers to the delay between recognizing the need for resources and having those resources available for actual use. This includes processing delays, settlement lags, search for counterparties, legal formalities, transfer restrictions, withdrawal schedules, and staged liquidation requirements. Timing friction means value can be real yet too slow.

At a first level, timing friction converts potential support into delayed support. The system may possess enough nominal value to bridge a problem in principle, but if the asset cannot convert before obligations mature, penalties escalate, or options collapse, that support fails in operational terms. Time therefore separates eventual solvency from immediate survivability. A system can be solvent on paper and still unstable because its assets move too slowly relative to its obligations.

At a deeper level, timing friction interacts with prior mechanisms to amplify fragility. If expenses cluster, if income is interrupted, or if obligations are fixed, the tolerance window narrows. Under those conditions, even moderate conversion delays become structurally significant. What matters is not the absolute conversion time alone, but the relationship between conversion time and system runway. An asset with a thirty-day conversion pathway may be functional in a system with long tolerance and irrelevant in a system with five-day pressure. Timing friction is therefore not a static trait. It becomes dangerous when it exceeds the interval the system can absorb without access.

The incorrect interpretation treats convertibility as a binary condition: either an asset can be sold or it cannot. This misses the central issue. Many assets are technically convertible but practically unusable because the conversion occurs too slowly, too unevenly, or with too much procedural dependence. The system then overcounts them as support because eventual access is mistaken for timely access.

Across multiple cycles, systems often reinforce reliance on slow-conversion assets because timing friction remains invisible until tested. The asset appears protective so long as no immediate need arises. Stable periods allow the belief that eventual access is sufficient. But every cycle that passes without testing timing increases the risk of future miscalculation, because the system's obligations may grow faster than its immediate liquidity while its stored value remains increasingly delayed in form.

A second expansion reveals failure emergence conditions more sharply. When the required interval of support becomes shorter than the asset's conversion path, the resource effectively disappears from the survival layer of the system. It still exists in ownership terms, and it may still carry full valuation, but it cannot prevent near-term instability. This is the key structural insight: timing friction can convert owned value into non-functional value without any change in legal ownership or nominal price. The asset is present but absent in operational time.

Illiquid assets become especially problematic during crisis conditions because the conditions that create the need for liquidity are often the same conditions that make illiquid assets harder to use. Crisis compresses time, reduces optionality, and weakens the conversion environment. This can occur at the individual level, the broader market level, or both simultaneously. Under such conditions, the difference between asset ownership and accessible liquidity becomes widest.

At a first level, crisis changes the usability profile of assets. Buyers become fewer, transaction confidence falls, price discovery weakens, and institutions or counterparties impose more cautious terms. Assets that appeared monetizable in stable conditions may require steep discounts, extended timelines, or partial realization. The system is then forced to confront not just illiquidity, but crisis illiquidity, where both speed and value deteriorate together.

At a deeper level, crisis produces correlation between need and inaccessibility. The system needs liquidity precisely when the asset is least willing to become liquid. This is a structural asymmetry. Under ordinary conditions, illiquidity may appear tolerable because there is no urgent demand for conversion. Under crisis, urgent demand appears at the same time that access quality worsens. This means the system cannot assume that yesterday's conversion pathway will remain open tomorrow. Illiquidity is not constant across states; it often intensifies at the exact moment reliance on it increases.

The incorrect interpretation assumes that large nominal assets provide security in crisis because they can be liquidated if necessary. This rests on calm-condition assumptions about price and access. In crisis, both assumptions are unstable. Assets may still be saleable, but only under delays or discounts that destroy their protective function. The issue is not that the asset vanishes. The issue is that it stops behaving like a reliable source of emergency support.

Across multiple cycles, crisis conditions also reveal how reliance on illiquid assets can become structurally embedded. Systems that repeatedly experience calm valuation growth may allocate more and more value into forms that enhance long-term worth while weakening near-term accessibility. This creates increasing divergence between represented strength and survival strength. When crisis finally tests the structure, the asset base cannot defend the system in proportion to its size because too much of it resides outside the accessible layer.

A second pass shows lock-in and threshold effects. Once a crisis begins, attempts to convert illiquid assets may themselves worsen outcomes by forcing distressed timing, unfavorable pricing, or incomplete access. The system may then consume its limited liquid reserves while waiting for conversion that arrives too late or at too great a loss. Failure emerges not because the system lacked assets, but because the assets belonged to the wrong access class for crisis survival. The balance sheet remained substantial while the survival layer failed.

Systems routinely overestimate available resources by conflating ownership with access. This overestimation is not a minor accounting issue. It is a structural distortion that affects obligation sizing, liquidity margins, tolerance for volatility, and interpretation of stability. When all owned value is mentally counted as available support, the system appears to possess more immediate resilience than it actually does. This miscalculation can remain invisible for long periods because ordinary operation does not require full conversion testing.

At a first level, overestimation occurs because nominal asset totals are easier to observe than access pathways. Statements, valuations, and account summaries provide clean numbers. Accessibility is messier. It requires asking how fast, how reliably, under what conditions, in what amount, and at what cost value can become usable. Because these questions are more complex and less visible, the system often defaults to the simpler measure. Total value becomes a proxy for available support.

At a deeper level, this distortion affects structure long before any failure occurs. The system may accept higher fixed obligations, smaller liquidity reserves, denser expense structures, or more concentrated income dependency because it believes its asset base provides fallback coverage. The problem is not simply misdescription. It is misconfiguration. Once overestimated resources are embedded into tolerance assumptions, the entire system operates on a false picture of survivability. That false picture persists until an access test occurs.

The incorrect interpretation treats net worth and accessible support as interchangeable indicators of strength. This leads to confidence during calm periods, because the system's represented resources are large. Yet calm periods do not test accessibility. They only preserve the illusion that all resources remain available. When stress arrives, the gap between counted resources and reachable resources becomes visible, often suddenly. The system then discovers that much of what it believed it could use was only ownable, not deployable.

Across repeated cycles, this overestimation can intensify. Each cycle without conversion failure strengthens the belief that owned assets are dependable reserves. The system's structure then leans harder on inaccessible value. More commitments are tolerated. Less attention is given to immediate liquidity. The divergence between nominal strength and operational resilience widens incrementally. By the time a stress event reveals the gap, the system may already be deeply dependent on resources that cannot arrive in time.

A second expansion reveals the lock-in effect more clearly. Once obligations, timing needs, and risk tolerance are calibrated against overstated resource availability, reducing that assumption becomes structurally difficult. The system has already been built around it. This means the overestimation does not merely produce one bad forecast; it shapes the operating architecture itself. Failure surface conditions then become clear: when obligations require near-term liquidity, when asset conversion faces friction or constraint, and when the system discovers that nominal wealth cannot substitute for accessible funds, instability emerges despite apparent abundance.

The mechanism therefore resolves into a final structural distinction. Survival is not defined by what the system owns in aggregate. It is defined by what the system can actually reach, convert, and deploy inside the time window that stress allows. Accessible liquidity determines whether obligations can be met, whether options remain open, and whether pressure can be absorbed without forced breakdown. Nominal asset value may influence longer-term recovery, future positioning, or eventual solvency, but it does not govern immediate survival unless it can cross the boundary into usable form when needed. The decisive variable is not possession of value, but access to value under pressure.

The Structural Weakness Mechanism

The Structural Weakness Mechanism defines weakness as an embedded property of system design rather than as an outcome created by events. A structurally weak system is not one that has already failed. It is one that is configured in a way that amplifies disturbance rather than absorbing it. Weakness therefore exists prior to disruption. It is present in the arrangement of the system's components, dependencies, margins, and pathways of interaction. Stress does not manufacture this weakness. Stress reveals it by forcing the system to respond under conditions where its hidden amplification tendencies become active.

At a first level, structural weakness can be understood as latent amplification potential. A system may appear orderly, stable, and functional while carrying internal properties that convert modest disturbances into disproportionate outcomes. These properties are not necessarily visible during low-stress periods because they do not produce immediate failure signals. They remain dormant until pressure enters the system. This is why weakness must be separated from visible breakdown. Failure is an event in observed time. Weakness is a condition in underlying structure. The two are related, but they are not identical.

The core properties that produce structural weakness are embedded in configuration. Coupling density determines how tightly one component's state affects another. Dependency concentration determines how much of the system relies on narrow channels or singular nodes. Margin compression determines how little space exists between normal operation and constraint. Lack of redundancy determines whether the system has alternative pathways when one component fails or degrades. Each of these conditions reduces damping capacity and increases propagation capacity. They do not need to generate immediate problems in order to matter. Their relevance lies in how they shape the system's response once disturbance begins.

Strength, in structural terms, is the ability to dampen propagation. A strong system may still experience shocks, interruptions, or pressure, but it prevents those disturbances from spreading rapidly across the whole structure. Weakness is the opposite tendency. It is the tendency for local pressure to travel, intensify, and interact with other sensitivities. This means that weakness is not merely low capacity in isolation. It is a multiplier embedded in the pathways of the system. It governs what happens after the initial disturbance enters.

A second pass into the mechanism reveals why structural weakness is often misread. Systems are frequently evaluated under ordinary operating conditions, where low variance and continuous support make internal design flaws difficult to detect. A tightly coupled system can appear efficient. A dependency-concentrated system can appear streamlined. A margin-compressed system can appear optimized. A low-redundancy structure can appear disciplined. Under low stress, these same design features may even improve apparent performance because they reduce slack and simplify flow. The problem is that the features producing apparent efficiency in calm conditions are often the same features that magnify disturbance when conditions change.

This creates a persistent observational distortion. The system is judged by visible output rather than by the shape of its response function. Because nothing has failed, weakness is assumed absent. Yet the absence of visible failure only means that the structure has not been tested beyond its current limits. It does not indicate that those limits are wide. Structural weakness therefore remains largely invisible until the system is forced to absorb a disturbance that exceeds its dampening capacity. At that point, what had seemed like stability reveals itself as conditional stability supported by uninterrupted calm.

This is why weakness must be treated as a multiplier rather than as an event category. A structurally weak system does not merely experience disturbance. It scales disturbance upward. A given input enters the structure, and the weakness determines how much larger the resulting outcome becomes. This multiplier effect is embedded in configuration long before any specific event occurs. The event is only the trigger that makes the multiplier visible. Weakness becomes legible when small disturbances produce outcomes that appear excessive relative to their initial size.

Small disruptions can create disproportionate outcomes because the magnitude of the result is not determined by the magnitude of the input alone. It is determined by the interaction between the input and the structure receiving it. In a robust system, a small shock tends to remain small. It is absorbed, contained, or diffused before it can propagate broadly. In a weak system, the same small shock can cross a sensitive threshold, activate dependencies, and begin moving through tightly connected pathways. The eventual consequence can therefore exceed the scale of the original disturbance by a wide margin.

At a first level, disproportion means that the output is larger than the input would appear to justify. The disturbance may be minor in nominal terms, but the system reacts as if it were much larger because the structure translates it into broader internal pressure. This is why identical events produce different outcomes across systems. The explanation is not hidden in the event itself. It is hidden in the structure receiving the event. One system dampens. Another amplifies.

The contrast between robust and weak structures becomes clearest here. A robust system has enough margin, segmentation, and redundancy to prevent local disturbances from crossing into wider instability. The disturbance enters, but its energy is dissipated. A weak system lacks these dampening properties. It transfers the disturbance forward through dependencies, compressed margins, and rigid sequences. The same small event therefore does not stay local. It becomes a structural test that the system fails because the pathways of amplification were already in place.

A second pass reveals that disproportion emerges through threshold behavior. The disturbance does not need to be large if the system is already operating near limits. Small inputs become dangerous when they push a compressed structure across boundaries that matter. A narrow liquidity margin, a tightly scheduled expense sequence, a concentrated dependency, or a delayed inflow may all appear manageable until a minor additional pressure collapses the remaining tolerance. The resulting outcome looks surprising only if the preexisting sensitivity was ignored. In structural terms, the event was not unusually large. It simply arrived at a point where the system's tolerance had already thinned.

This means the event size is not the explanatory variable. The system's preexisting sensitivity is. Disproportion is not random escalation. It is the visible expression of embedded weakness. The event is a probe. The structure determines the reading. Once this is recognized, small disruptions stop being interpreted as anomalies that somehow "caused too much damage." Instead, they are recognized as disturbances that encountered a system whose thresholds were already too close to normal operating pressure.

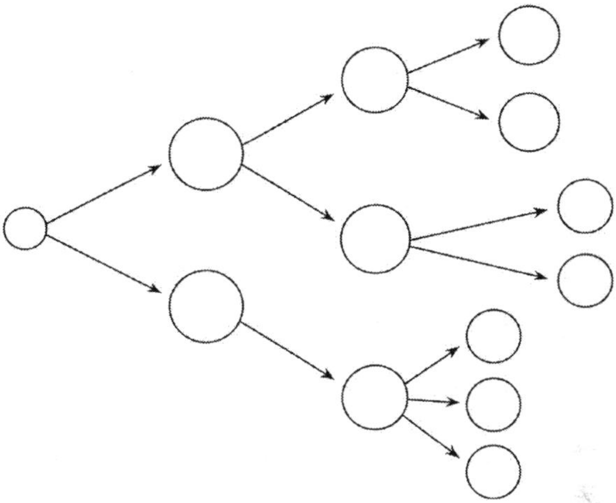

[Figure 4: Structural Weakness Amplification Model]

Amplification is not accidental. It is produced by specific design flaws that determine how pressure moves once it enters the system. Structural amplification can be defined as the multiplication of disturbance through internal pathways. The system does not simply register the initial event and stop there. It transmits that event through its architecture, increasing either the speed, scale, or persistence of the resulting pressure. Tight coupling, single-point dependencies, lack of buffering, and sequential fragility are among the primary design flaws that create these pathways.

Tight coupling means that components are so closely linked that changes in one state rapidly alter adjacent states. This reduces the time available for isolation or adjustment. Single-point dependencies mean that one node, source, or channel carries a disproportionate share of system function. If that node weakens, the whole structure feels the effect immediately. Lack of buffering means there is too little reserve or separation between components to absorb pressure locally. Sequential fragility means that processes depend on a narrow order of operations, so delay or disruption in one step disturbs all subsequent steps. Each flaw shapes not only whether propagation occurs, but how quickly and how far it moves.

At a first level, these flaws determine the path, speed, and scale of disturbance transmission. A tightly coupled structure accelerates movement. A dependency-concentrated structure deepens impact. A low-buffer structure reduces absorption. A sequentially fragile structure turns delay into accumulation. Together, they form the channels through which pressure stops being local and becomes systemic. The system is not merely affected by disturbance. It is built to carry disturbance inward.

A second pass is required here because amplification rarely arises from one flaw alone. Design flaws interact. A system with tight coupling and low buffering will propagate pressure faster than a system with only one of those properties. A system with single-point dependency and sequential fragility will not only experience interruption but also an ordered collapse of downstream functions. This interaction produces amplification chains. A disturbance enters one component, passes through dependency structure, encounters compressed margins, then escalates because adjacent components have insufficient separation. The result is not a single propagation event but a sequence: disturbance, transmission, accumulation, escalation.

This interaction makes amplification deterministic rather than accidental. Once the structure is known, the likely path of propagation becomes intelligible. It may not be possible to predict the precise triggering event, but it is possible to see that certain disturbances will not remain local because the design leaves them no such path. Weakness is therefore not vagueness or fragility in a general sense. It is the specific arrangement that causes disturbances to multiply rather than dissipate.

A further layer appears when these flaws become normalized through repeated calm cycles. Efficient operation under low stress often encourages tighter coupling, less redundancy, and thinner margins because those properties can improve apparent performance. Over time, the system begins to reward the very features that later create amplification. What appears as refinement in calm conditions becomes transmission architecture in stressed conditions. The structure is therefore shaped not only by technical design but by the repeated reinforcement of calm-state efficiency. This is one reason amplification can be so surprising when it appears. The system was optimized for ordinary flow and, in doing so, embedded its own escalation pathways.

Amplification depends on where weakness exists within the structure. This brings the mechanism to the distinction between weak links and strong links. A weak link is the point at which failure propagates most easily. It is the component, node, timing window, or dependency channel with the lowest tolerance relative to the pressure it must absorb. A strong link is the opposite: a point with high tolerance, effective buffering, and low transmission risk. System stability is governed not by the average of these conditions but by the minimum-bound point where pressure can most easily break through.

At a first level, this means that overall system strength cannot be inferred from isolated areas of resilience. A system may have several strong components and still remain vulnerable if one weak link sits in a critical location. That weak link can dominate behavior because pressure does not need to break the whole structure uniformly. It only needs to move through the most vulnerable route. Once that route opens, strong areas elsewhere may do little to prevent the resulting propagation if they are not positioned to isolate it.

This is why distributed strength differs from concentrated strength. A system with many moderately strong components and no severe weak link may outperform a system with several very strong areas but one critical point of concentrated weakness. The latter looks stronger on average, but the average is misleading. The weak link sets the threshold. It determines how much disturbance the system can absorb before local failure begins to travel.

A second pass reveals why strengthening already strong areas has limited structural effect. Additional resilience added to parts of the system that were not governing failure thresholds may improve local performance, but it does not materially change the point where the system is most likely to break. If the weak link remains unchanged, the failure surface remains largely unchanged. This is a structural asymmetry. Gains in strong zones often produce diminishing returns because they do not alter the minimum-bound condition. The system remains governed by the same narrow threshold even while other areas become more robust.

This also introduces the distinction between failure localization and propagation risk. A weak link is not dangerous solely because it may fail. Its real danger depends on whether its failure remains confined or travels. A weak component in an isolated structure may create inconvenience without system-wide instability. A weak component embedded in dense dependency and feedback pathways becomes a governing threat because local weakness can no longer stay local. The importance of the weak link is therefore determined both by its low tolerance and by its connectivity to the rest of the structure.

Weak links become significantly more dangerous when embedded in feedback structures. Feedback loops transform one-time disturbances into repeated escalation. A feedback loop exists when outputs re-enter the system as inputs, altering subsequent behavior. Some feedback loops are stabilizing. They counteract deviation and restore balance. Others are destabilizing. They reinforce deviation, causing an initial disturbance to grow rather than recede. The Structural Weakness Mechanism is concerned with the latter because reinforcing loops convert structural weakness into self-accelerating instability.

At a first level, destabilizing feedback means that the system's response to disruption increases the disruption itself. The initial disturbance is no longer the only source of pressure. The system begins generating additional pressure internally through its own reaction pathways. What started as an external or local problem becomes partly endogenous. The system is now helping the disturbance continue.

A simple structural pattern appears here. Disturbance produces strain. Strain triggers responses within the system. Those responses narrow capacity, reduce flexibility, or intensify coupling. The reduced capacity then magnifies the next round of strain. The loop feeds itself. Pressure is no longer moving in a straight line from event to outcome. It is cycling. Each cycle returns to the system with more destabilizing force than before.

A second pass shows that feedback changes the tempo of failure progression. Without feedback, propagation can still occur, but it tends to remain tied to the original disturbance and the structure's passive transmission pathways. With reinforcing feedback, escalation accelerates because each stage creates conditions for the next stage to be worse. The system does not merely transmit the original shock; it compounds it. A modest loss of flexibility can force more rigid decisions, which then create new constraints, which then intensify the original problem. Disturbance becomes self-reinforcing.

This matters because once feedback begins, containment becomes more difficult even if the initial event has stopped expanding. The structure keeps producing secondary pressure. The system is no longer dealing with a static disruption but with an evolving internal process. This is why feedback loops often mark the difference between serious stress and accelerating instability. They convert vulnerability from a structural property into a dynamic process that unfolds across repeated cycles.

The danger increases further when feedback intersects with weak links and amplification pathways already described. A weak link allows local failure to begin. Amplification pathways move that failure through the structure. Feedback ensures that each stage of movement worsens the conditions of the next stage. The combination is what turns fragility into cascade. Weakness is no longer passive. It becomes self-propelling once disruption passes a critical point.

Once amplification and feedback combine, local failures stop remaining contained. A local failure is a breakdown at a single node, component, or operating point within the system. On its own, this need not be system-threatening. Whether it remains local or becomes systemic depends on the surrounding structure. In systems with segmentation, buffering, and low dependency concentration, local failure can often be isolated. In weak structures, it rarely stays in place. It spreads through dependencies, coupling channels, and reinforcing feedback until wider system behavior is altered.

At a first level, propagation occurs because local nodes are rarely fully independent. One component supports another, one sequence depends on a prior one, one obligation is timed against another, or one resource channel sustains several downstream commitments. When the local node weakens, all connected elements inherit pressure. If those connected elements are already operating with low margin or high rigidity, the pressure intensifies rather than dissipates. The local failure thus becomes the first step in a broader chain.

This chain can be described structurally as node to subsystem to system-wide consequence. The initial weakness appears in one location, then disrupts the subsystem that depends on it, and finally alters whole-system behavior when enough connected functions are affected. The scale of the consequence is therefore determined by connectivity. A poorly connected weak node may fail without broad damage. A highly connected weak node becomes a cascade origin point. Again, the event itself is not the central explanatory variable. The topology of the structure is.

A second pass shows why containment fails in weak structures. Containment requires available boundaries. The system must possess slack, segmentation, or alternate routes that allow pressure to stop moving. Weak structures lack these boundaries. Tight coupling carries the disturbance forward too quickly. Dependency concentration means too many components rely on the failed point. Margin compression leaves too little room for localized adaptation. Feedback loops magnify the effect before the system can stabilize. By the time the failure is recognized, it is already no longer local in functional terms.

This produces failure chains whose severity is not proportional to the size of the first break. A minor interruption at one node may trigger a moderate subsystem problem, which then activates wider constraints, leading to system-wide destabilization. The final outcome appears far larger than the initiating event because the structure connected local weakness to broad consequence. Cascade is therefore structural, not accidental. It is the expression of a system built without adequate dampening boundaries between parts that matter.

Across repeated cycles, systems that survive local failures without explicit collapse may still become weaker. Each contained-but-costly episode can consume margin, increase coupling reliance elsewhere, or reduce redundancy. If those losses are not structurally restored, the next local failure begins from a more compressed state. This means cascade risk can increase over time even when past failures seemed manageable. The system learns the wrong lesson from survival. It interprets non-collapse as structural adequacy, while actual tolerance may be narrowing beneath the surface.

The final structural principle follows directly from this progression. Amplification is not event-driven. It is design-driven. The same disturbance can produce radically different outcomes depending on how the system is built. Where weakness exists, how that weakness connects to other components, and whether feedback loops are available to reinforce disruption together determine the system's behavior under stress. The disturbance enters from outside or emerges locally, but the scale of the consequence is set by the architecture receiving it.

A system therefore carries its future stress behavior inside its present configuration. Stress does not improvise the response. It activates it. The pathways of amplification, the governing weak links, the presence or absence of containment boundaries, and the availability of reinforcing loops are already embedded before the triggering event arrives. Once activated, they determine whether disturbance will remain local, become subsystem pressure, or expand into whole-system instability.

Risk, then, is not defined by what enters the system. It is defined by how the system is built to respond.

The Single Point of Failure Mechanism

The Single Point of Failure Mechanism describes a structural condition in which a disproportionate share of system continuity depends on one component, channel, or function. A single point of failure is not merely a dependency. All systems contain dependencies. It becomes structurally significant when the failure of one node disrupts a broad portion of total operation. The defining feature is therefore not existence but concentration. A node becomes critical when too much of the system's ability to function, replenish, sequence, or stabilize passes through it. Its importance is measured by the scale of disruption produced by its absence, not by how visible or probable that absence appears under normal conditions.

A critical dependency node can take several forms. It may be a single income source through which most inflow enters the system. It may be a single liquidity channel through which obligations are bridged and timing gaps are managed. It may be a single operational pathway on which multiple processes depend for execution. It may also be a single timing dependency where one scheduled event or one narrow interval determines whether a larger sequence can continue. These forms differ in substance, but they share the same structural property: functional concentration. They hold more of the system's continuity than their singular appearance suggests.

At a first level, the distinction between distributed and centralized dependency clarifies the mechanism. In a distributed system, multiple channels share functional load. No single node governs a disproportionate share of total continuity. Failure in one area reduces performance, but the system continues operating through alternate routes or partially preserved capacity. In a centralized system, by contrast, one node carries enough load that its disruption changes the state of the whole structure. The system is not merely inconvenienced. It becomes unstable because the node was governing too much of what had to continue.

Not all dependencies are equal because not all carry equal concentration. A system may rely on one component for a marginal function and on another for a critical one. What defines a single point of failure is the degree of dependence embedded in the node relative to the amount of disturbance its failure creates. This means criticality must be measured in terms of impact, not nominal centrality alone. A node may appear ordinary in stable conditions because it does not visibly dominate daily observation. Yet it can still be structurally dominant if its removal disables a wide range of downstream functions.

A second pass into the mechanism reveals that nodes become critical through load concentration, not simply through singularity. A component can exist alone without being a single point of failure if little depends on it or if its function is easily replaced. Conversely, a node can become critical over time because more and more load is routed through it. Stable operation encourages concentration. As a system experiences repeated cycles without disruption, it often assigns more responsibility to the same reliable channel. More obligations are calibrated against one inflow source. More timing assumptions are anchored to one recurring event. More operational sequencing is built around one route that has "always worked." Criticality grows through repeated dependence.

This is why a node can appear stable while becoming structurally dominant. Stability of the node does not reduce its criticality. It may increase it, because uninterrupted function encourages the rest of the system to lean more heavily on it. Over time, the node becomes less one dependency among many and more the governing dependency around which the rest of the structure is arranged. The system's apparent confidence rises with repeated stability, while its actual fragility increases because failure impact is becoming more concentrated.

Criticality, then, is defined by impact of failure rather than probability of failure. A node may have low observed failure frequency and still be the most dangerous point in the structure. If its disruption produces disproportionate system-wide consequences, it remains a single point of failure regardless of how calm its history appears. This establishes the transition forward. Systems do not generally fail everywhere at once. They fail where dependency has been most tightly concentrated and where tolerance is narrowest relative to what that point is required to carry.

Systems fail at their most constrained point because system behavior is governed by minimum-bound conditions rather than by averages. A constraint is the point where tolerance is lowest relative to the demand placed upon it. It is the narrowest part of the structure, the place where capacity is thinnest, flexibility is most limited, or replacement options are weakest. The rest of the system may appear strong in aggregate, but overall stability is not determined by average strength. It is determined by the point that cannot absorb the next increment of pressure.

At a first level, this can be understood through limiting-factor behavior. A system may contain several strong subsystems and still remain vulnerable if one constrained node sits in a critical pathway. Pressure does not distribute itself according to where capacity is highest. It accumulates where capacity is smallest relative to demand. This is why highly functional systems can still break abruptly. Their weakness is not visible in average performance because the governing condition lies at the narrowest point, not across the whole structure.

The contrast between strong subsystems and a constrained node is essential here. A system may have strong income, substantial assets, or orderly operations in many areas, yet remain fragile if one timing dependency, one liquidity window, or one centralized obligation channel has very little margin. The strong parts do not cancel the weak point. They coexist with it. When stress arrives, the system does not fail according to its strongest zones or even its average condition. It fails where the load meets the thinnest capacity.

A second pass reveals bottleneck behavior more precisely. The constrained point acts like the narrowest section in a flow system. Total throughput is limited not by the widest channels, but by the narrowest one that all flow must traverse. As demand rises or conditions tighten, pressure accumulates behind this narrow point. The rest of the structure may retain unused capacity, but that unused capacity does not resolve the bottleneck if it cannot bypass it. Failure thus emerges where margin is thinnest, not where activity is highest. The most active zone may continue functioning until the constrained node breaks, at which point the larger system loses continuity because the governing restriction was never elsewhere.

This minimum-bound logic also explains why systems often appear resilient right up to the moment they do not. The broader structure may contain enough visible strength to disguise the fact that one zone is operating near its limits. Because that constrained point continues functioning, its risk remains latent. Once a modest disturbance enters, however, it is the narrow point that governs the result. The disturbance does not need to overwhelm the whole system. It only needs to exceed the smallest effective margin along the most critical route.

Across repeated cycles, constraint points often become more important because success tends to preserve them. If the system continues operating, the narrow point is assumed adequate. More flow is then routed through it, more timing is synchronized around it, or more functions are built to depend on it. The result is not relaxation of the constraint but entrenchment of it. The system becomes increasingly governed by the same minimum-capacity zone. This leads directly to the next condition. Constraints become dangerous when there is no alternative pathway around them.

Redundancy is the structural availability of alternative pathways, substitutes, or backup functions that allow the system to continue operating when one route is disrupted. Redundancy is not excess in the casual sense, and it is not inefficiency by definition. It is the system property that permits rerouting under pressure. Without redundancy, the failure of a critical node becomes immediate functional disruption because there is nowhere else for the required load to go. The system moves from continuity to discontinuity in a binary way.

At a first level, redundancy means the system can preserve function even if one component weakens or fails. The substitute does not need to be identical in quality or scale. What matters is continuity of operation. A system with alternative pathways can degrade without collapsing. A system without them remains dependent on uninterrupted performance of the primary route. This is why redundancy changes the nature of failure. It does not merely reduce the probability that a node fails. It changes what happens if failure occurs.

Without redundancy, systems are binary. They are working or not working, funded or unfunded, flowing or stalled. The failure of the single path is not partially absorbed because no alternate route exists to preserve the function. This creates sharp transitions rather than gradual degradation. A system with redundancy can experience local failure and continue in reduced form. A system without redundancy often experiences local failure as immediate system interruption because the failed node was also the only node capable of carrying that function.

A second pass clarifies the deeper structural role of redundancy. The importance of redundancy is not only that it provides backup presence, but that it reduces propagation when a failure occurs. In a multi-path system, disruption can be rerouted, slowed, isolated, or diluted. In a single-path system, the failure pressure has only one route: straight into the rest of the structure. Redundancy therefore changes the geometry of propagation. It introduces spacing and substitution, which reduce the chance that one node's failure becomes a whole-system event.

This is why redundancy should not be confused with simple surplus. Its structural value lies in preserving continuity under disruption. A system may look lean and efficient without redundancy, but that apparent efficiency is conditional on uninterrupted operation. Once the primary route breaks, the absence of alternatives becomes immediately visible. The system discovers that what appeared streamlined was actually binary in design.

Across multiple cycles, systems that lack redundancy often normalize this binary condition because uninterrupted function conceals the absence of alternatives. If the single path continues to work, the lack of redundancy is easy to ignore. The system begins to rely on continued success rather than on structural continuity. Over time, this reliance becomes embedded in obligations, schedules, and expectations. The failure surface narrows further because the system has built around a route that it cannot afford to lose and cannot replace if it does.

This moves the mechanism forward into fragility through dependency centralization. Centralization occurs when multiple functions rely on a single node or pathway. It increases fragility not because resources are absent, but because access to those resources or functions is routed through too little structure. The more the system depends on one node, the more that node governs outcomes. Fragility emerges from over-reliance, not necessarily from scarcity.

At a first level, centralization concentrates load. More functions, more timing commitments, or more operational flows are passed through one dependency. This increases efficiency under calm conditions because coordination becomes simpler and flow can be more direct. A centralized node often appears valuable precisely because it supports so much with so little visible friction. The system experiences concentration as convenience and coherence.

Yet centralization also increases sensitivity to disruption. Because more functions rely on the same node, its interruption affects a broader portion of the structure. A problem that would have remained local in a distributed system now becomes systemic because the centralized node was carrying too many responsibilities at once. The node's operational significance grows faster than its singular appearance suggests. As more reliance accumulates, the impact of its failure grows non-linearly. It is not simply that one more function depends on it. It is that each added dependency increases the number of interactions and sequences that can be disturbed when the node weakens.

A second pass into centralization reveals the efficiency trade-off more clearly. Centralization improves flow during calm conditions because it reduces coordination cost, consolidates management, and may increase apparent stability. But these same gains come from concentrating functional control. The system becomes cleaner in appearance and more fragile in response. The very structure that improves calm-state performance also enlarges failure impact under stress. This is why fragility should not be interpreted as the absence of strength. It can emerge inside systems that are highly resourced and apparently well-organized. The issue is not resource quantity but dependency arrangement.

Scaling fragility follows from this. As reliance on the centralized node grows, the consequence of disruption grows more than proportionally. More functions are affected, more timing sequences are interrupted, and more secondary pressures are activated. The system's tolerance becomes increasingly dependent on one point remaining uninterrupted. This dependence often deepens gradually and invisibly, especially when prior cycles have been stable. Each cycle of reliable performance justifies routing more through the same node. Centralization thus reinforces itself until the system's broader behavior is effectively governed by one dependency.

Once centralized, failure does not remain local because the connection structure already links the node to multiple downstream functions. This creates failure pathways. A failure pathway is the sequence through which disruption spreads from a node to dependent components, then to larger subsystems, and finally to the wider structure. The pathway is not created by the failure event itself. It is created by the way dependencies, timing, and resources are connected in advance.

At a first level, node failure causes dependent functions to lose continuity. A missed inflow interrupts obligations timed against it. A blocked liquidity channel prevents bridging across required intervals. A stalled operational route delays subsequent actions that depend on prior completion. These downstream effects are not separate events. They are the extension of the original node failure through the system's connection map. The failure spreads because the node was embedded inside multiple sequences.

Timing dependencies are a primary transmission route. If one event must occur before another can proceed, delay at the origin cascades forward through the sequence. Resource dependencies are another route. If several functions draw from one source, interruption at that source reduces all of them at once. Sequential processes add further pressure because delay or failure in one stage can idle, disrupt, or invalidate later stages. The system thus experiences propagation not as a mysterious chain reaction but as the predictable unfolding of preexisting dependency order.

A second pass reveals how cascade chains form in centralized systems. The node fails first. Then a subsystem that depended on it loses continuity. Then the broader system becomes unstable because multiple subsystems are simultaneously impaired or because the failure of one critical sequence blocks several others. The chain can be described as node to subsystem to system. What makes this chain accelerate is centralization itself. In a distributed system, failure paths are shorter, narrower, and easier to isolate. In a centralized system, the failed node sits upstream from too many functions, so propagation expands rapidly before containment can occur.

This is also where node strength must be separated from containment capacity. A node may be strong in normal operation and still dangerous as a central dependency because the issue is not only how often it fails, but what happens if it does. Containment depends on decoupling, alternate routes, and distributed function. If those are absent, even a relatively strong node remains a structural threat because its rare failure would be catastrophic. This returns the analysis to impact rather than probability. The single point of failure is defined by consequence structure.

Across repeated cycles, centralized systems often reinforce their own failure pathways. If the node continues to perform, more functions become synchronized around it. More timing dependencies are added, more resources are routed through it, and more subsystems assume its continuity. The pathway becomes denser with each cycle of calm. When failure finally occurs, it does not enter a static structure. It enters one that has been progressively shaped to make the consequences broader and faster. This is why single-point failures can appear sudden while actually being years in the making. The triggering event is sudden. The dependence architecture is cumulative.

Preventing the structural consequences of these pathways is not a matter of eliminating dependency altogether. No system removes failure risk completely. The governing principle is distribution. Robustness arises when dependency is spread across multiple channels, timing routes, or functional sources so that failure impact can be diluted rather than concentrated. Distribution does not mean the system becomes invulnerable. It means that no single disruption governs too large a share of total continuity.

This clarifies the final structural principle. Systems do not fail because they have dependencies. Dependencies are unavoidable. They fail because too much depends on too little. When critical functions are concentrated into one income channel, one liquidity route, one timing event, or one operational path, the system's survival becomes tied to uninterrupted performance at a singular point. Distribution changes this relationship. It reduces load concentration, lowers cascade risk, and weakens the amplification of local failure by ensuring that the structure does not hand control of the whole system to one node.

Robustness, then, is not the elimination of disruption. It is the distribution of consequence. A distributed system can lose one path and continue. A centralized system can lose one path and stop. The difference lies not in whether disturbance occurs, but in how widely critical functions are spread before disturbance arrives. Stability is determined by how the system allocates dependency across its structure, and whether continuity can survive the loss of any one route without crossing into broader failure. Systems do not fail because they contain risk. They fail because functional concentration allows one break to matter too much.

The Concentration Mechanism

The Concentration Mechanism describes a structural condition in which too much system function depends on too few inputs, channels, or resources. Concentration is not scarcity. A system may possess substantial income, significant asset value, and large nominal capacity while still being highly concentrated. The issue is not how much exists in aggregate, but how narrowly system continuity is distributed across what exists. When function is compressed into a limited set of inputs, each input carries a disproportionate share of total continuity. Dependency per input rises as the number of inputs falls. This is the foundation of the mechanism. Fragility emerges not because the system lacks resources, but because the distribution of reliance across those resources is too narrow.

At a first level, concentration can be understood as distribution imbalance. If a wide set of inputs supports system operation, the burden carried by any one input is limited. If only a few inputs support that same operation, each input becomes more structurally important. Its continuity matters more because more of the system is attached to it. This applies across multiple domains. Income concentration appears when inflow depends on a small number of sources. Asset concentration appears when stored value is held in a narrow range of forms. Liquidity concentration appears when access to usable funds depends on limited channels or timing windows. Operational concentration appears when essential processes depend on a small set of pathways, counterparties, or nodes. In each case, the mechanism is the same: narrowing the distribution of support increases the load carried by each remaining support point.

This distinction matters because concentrated systems often appear strong while conditions remain uninterrupted. A narrow structure can be easier to track, easier to manage, and easier to interpret. The simplicity of the arrangement can create the impression that the system is efficient and coherent. But this coherence is conditional. The fewer the inputs, the fewer the independent sources of support. This means that each disruption has a larger potential effect because it strikes a structure that has allowed individual inputs to become structurally dominant. Concentration therefore increases consequence per failure event. The same event that would produce limited damage in a distributed system produces larger damage in a concentrated one because more of the system is attached to what fails.

A deeper pass into the mechanism shows that over-reliance rarely appears suddenly. It develops gradually through repeated success. When a small set of inputs functions reliably across multiple cycles, the system interprets that reliability as adequacy. More obligations are then calibrated to the same inflow sources. More value is stored in the same asset forms. More operating continuity is built around the same channels. Stability encourages further concentration because uninterrupted performance makes additional distribution seem unnecessary. As a result, concentration is often the byproduct of prior stability rather than of visible disorder. The system becomes more concentrated because its existing narrow structure has not yet been punished by disruption.

This repeated-cycle dynamic is critical because it explains why concentration often remains unrecognized. Each stable cycle validates the structure. A concentrated income stream appears dependable because it has continued. A concentrated asset base appears sufficient because valuation has remained intact. A concentrated liquidity channel appears usable because it has not yet been tested under pressure. The system then expands around this apparent dependability. The narrow structure becomes more deeply embedded, and dependency per input rises further. Concentration therefore compounds silently during calm periods. It is reinforced by the same conditions that conceal its danger.

A second pass reveals the deeper asymmetry. As concentration rises, the system does not merely become somewhat more exposed. It changes the consequence profile of interruption. Failure at any concentrated point now matters more because that point carries a larger fraction of total function. This means concentration increases fragility through consequence magnification. The system's headline resources may remain unchanged or even improve while structural tolerance declines. More value can exist, more inflow can occur, and more apparent stability can be observed, yet the system can still become more fragile because dependency is being compressed into fewer routes. Concentration is therefore a condition of structure, not a synonym for low resource quantity.

This concentration rarely exists in only one place. It appears across multiple layers of the system simultaneously. Income may be concentrated into a small number of inflow sources. Assets may be concentrated into narrow forms of stored value. Obligations may be concentrated into fixed commitments that assume the continuity of specific structures. Each layer has its own fragility profile, but their interaction is what gives the mechanism its full force. Concentration is not an isolated variable. It is a pattern that can span the input layer, the storage layer, and the demand layer at the same time.

Income concentration is the most immediate form because it governs replenishment. When inflow depends on only a few sources, the continuity of system support becomes highly sensitive to the condition of those sources. A disturbance in one source produces a larger proportionate decline in capacity because few alternatives exist to offset it. The system then confronts interruption not as a partial inconvenience distributed across many channels, but as a major reduction in total operating input.

The narrower the inflow structure, the more each source becomes a governing dependency.

Asset concentration introduces a different but related fragility. Here the issue is not the narrowness of inflow but the narrowness of stored value. If value is concentrated into a limited set of forms, then access, conversion, and preservation become dependent on the conditions attached to those forms. A system may possess substantial nominal wealth, but if that wealth is stored narrowly, then shifts affecting that narrow storage class can alter large portions of total resource position at once. The fragility lies not only in valuation sensitivity but in the loss of optionality. Few asset forms mean few alternative pathways for access, liquidation, or stability under changing conditions.

Obligation concentration completes the pattern. A system can concentrate its commitments by tying them to fixed structures, narrow timing assumptions, or specific support conditions. When obligations are dense, rigid, and attached to a limited set of sustaining inputs, the demand side of the structure becomes concentrated as well. This means the system is not only dependent on few inflows and narrow asset forms; it is also committed through obligations that assume those same concentrated supports will continue. The result is a system that is narrow at the point of replenishment, narrow at the point of stored value, and narrow at the point of required outflow.

Each of these layers independently increases fragility, but the full structural danger emerges when they combine. Concentrated income with fixed obligations creates timing fragility. If one inflow source is delayed or interrupted, obligations do not wait. Concentrated assets with low liquidity create access fragility. The system may hold value, but not in forms that can offset near-term stress. Concentrated obligations with concentrated income create alignment fragility because a small number of sustaining channels must continuously match a fixed pattern of demands. These layers do not simply add risk side by side. They reinforce one another. Weakness in one layer makes weakness in another more consequential.

A second pass into this interaction shows that concentration compounds because each layer reduces the system's ability to compensate for the others. If income is concentrated but assets are broad and liquid, the system retains some substitute capacity. If assets are concentrated but income is distributed and resilient, inflow may maintain continuity despite storage narrowness. If obligations are rigid but support layers are broad, the rigidity may remain tolerable. The problem emerges when narrowness exists across layers at once. Then the system loses compensation pathways. Income interruption cannot be offset because assets are narrow or inaccessible. Asset conversion delays matter more because obligations are fixed. Fixed obligations become more dangerous because inflow is narrow. Concentration therefore multiplies system sensitivity through cross-layer reinforcement. It compounds, not just adds.

This compounding effect means that concentration must be understood as an architecture rather than as a characteristic of one variable. The system becomes fragile not merely because one part is narrow, but because several parts are narrow in ways that align. The alignment creates coherent downside transmission. A disturbance entering one concentrated layer quickly encounters other layers that are also concentrated, leaving little room for dissipation. This leads directly to reduced tolerance to disruption.

Tolerance is the system's ability to absorb variation without entering instability. It is the amount of disturbance, delay, loss, or misalignment the structure can endure before its normal operating state begins to break down. Concentration narrows this tolerance because it reduces flexibility, substitution options, and recovery pathways. A system supported by many inputs can lose one and continue. A system supported by few inputs cannot make the same adjustment because each input already carries too much weight. The effect of concentration is therefore to reduce the number of ways the system can respond when disruption appears.

At a first level, fewer inputs mean fewer adjustment mechanisms. If one income source weakens in a distributed structure, others may continue supplying support. If one asset form becomes inaccessible, other stores of value may still remain usable. If one obligation pathway becomes strained, flexibility elsewhere may absorb part of the pressure. In a concentrated system, these alternate routes are limited. The structure has fewer substitutes available, so each disruption has a more direct path into core operations. Tolerance declines because the system cannot reroute stress easily.

Flexibility also narrows under concentration because narrow dependency encourages commitment around continuity assumptions. When support seems stable, obligations and processes are built more tightly against it. This makes the system look orderly during calm periods, but it reduces its ability to move when conditions change. A concentrated system therefore does not merely lack substitutes in static terms. It often becomes more rigid over time because its operating configuration is increasingly synchronized with its narrow support structure. Reduced tolerance is thus partly a function of insufficient alternatives and partly a function of how deeply the system has been built around the assumption that those few alternatives will not be needed.

A second pass shows that fragility enters through dependence chains. When support is concentrated, disruption at one point affects a large chain of connected functions. A break in one input is not isolated to that input. It affects timing, obligation fulfillment, access to liquidity, preservation of margin, and the ability to recover. The fewer the support points, the more each one sits upstream from broad portions of the system. This is why tolerance often shrinks before failure becomes visible. The system may continue operating, but it is doing so with fewer viable response pathways. Its apparent stability hides the fact that its ability to absorb the next variation has already been reduced.

This hidden contraction is important. Tolerance does not vanish only when visible failure occurs. It erodes as concentration rises. A system can remain functional while its capacity to absorb disruption steadily declines. Because no event has yet tested that reduced tolerance, the contraction is easy to ignore. But structurally, the system has already changed state. It has become more brittle. The next interruption does not need to be especially large. It only needs to meet a system whose range of adjustment has narrowed beyond what appearances suggest.

Across repeated cycles, this erosion can become self-reinforcing. Stable operation under concentration is often interpreted as evidence that tolerance remains wide. In reality, the system may simply not have encountered a test severe enough to expose its narrowed adjustment range. Each calm cycle then supports further compression. More dependence is loaded onto the same narrow supports, and tolerance shrinks further. The system becomes increasingly capable of appearing stable and increasingly incapable of absorbing variation. Reduced tolerance therefore arrives before visible instability, not after it.

This reduction in tolerance does not scale linearly. Fragility grows faster than concentration itself. Each increase in concentration raises dependency per input, decreases substitution options, and increases cascade risk. These changes interact, so the resulting vulnerability expands more than proportionally. A small increase in concentration can therefore produce a larger increase in fragility than a simple one-to-one comparison would suggest. The system is not merely becoming somewhat narrower. It is moving into a regime where each remaining input governs more of total continuity.

At a first level, the non-linearity comes from load concentration. When more function is routed through fewer supports, each support becomes more important than before. This alone increases failure consequence. But at the same time, substitution capacity is falling. The system cannot easily replace the lost support because fewer alternatives remain. In addition, propagation risk rises because broad parts of the structure now depend on the same points. These mechanisms do not sit separately. They reinforce each other. The support point becomes more important, harder to replace, and more connected to downstream continuity all at once. Fragility therefore accelerates.

This is why small increases in concentration can create large increases in vulnerability. The movement is not linear because the burden per input rises while the number of recovery pathways falls. At moderate concentration, the system may still retain enough substitutes to remain manageable. Beyond a certain point, however, the remaining supports become structurally dominant. Now each marginal increase in concentration produces a disproportionately large reduction in system resilience. The system crosses from having narrowness as a concern to having narrowness as the governing condition of survival.

A second pass reveals threshold behavior. Concentration can move the system across invisible limits where the nature of disruption changes. Below the threshold, interruptions remain manageable because residual substitutes and margin still exist. Above the threshold, similar interruptions trigger instability because the structure has lost enough distribution that local disturbances become system-level problems. This shift often appears abrupt, but it is structurally cumulative. The threshold was approached gradually as concentration rose. The visible jump occurs only when the accumulated narrowing becomes active under stress.

This threshold logic is essential because it shows why fragility accelerates rather than grows smoothly. The system does not merely become incrementally worse with each unit of concentration. It may remain apparently stable for a long period, then exhibit a sharp change in behavior once a critical level of distribution loss is reached. From that point forward, even moderate disturbances can generate severe outcomes because the structure is no longer broad enough to dissipate them. Concentration therefore produces non-linear downside exposure. The consequences of crossing the threshold exceed what a linear model would predict.

Despite this, concentration is often mistaken for efficiency. A concentrated structure can look simpler, cleaner, and easier to manage. Fewer inputs mean fewer moving parts. Fewer asset forms mean less visible complexity. Narrowly aligned obligations can produce orderly payment patterns and coherent routines. From a calm-condition perspective, this can appear optimized. The system looks disciplined because its structure is compact. It looks strong because there are fewer visible complications to manage.

At a first level, this perceived efficiency comes from reduced complexity. A concentrated system is easier to describe and easier to monitor. Relationships between inputs and outputs are clearer. Management burden appears lower because there are fewer channels to coordinate. Stable periods reinforce this perception because uninterrupted conditions allow the concentrated structure to operate without visible stress. As long as nothing breaks, the structure can appear elegant.

But this interpretation is misleading because efficiency in calm conditions is not the same as resilience under stress. The gains in calm-state simplicity often come from removing distribution and redundancy. That removal can improve apparent performance while uninterrupted conditions hold. Yet the hidden cost is that the system has fewer ways to respond when conditions do not hold. What looks optimized is therefore often condition-dependent stability. It is efficient only so long as the environment continues to validate its narrow structure.

A deeper pass shows that the stability illusion created by concentration is powerful because it is reinforced by success. Each calm cycle confirms that the simplified structure "works." This makes broader distribution appear unnecessary and can even make it look inefficient by comparison. The system then treats narrowness as competence rather than as exposure. The removal of alternate pathways feels like refinement. The concentration of value feels like focus. The tight alignment of obligations feels like control. Yet these benefits are contingent on uninterrupted conditions. They are not evidence that the system can withstand disruption.

A second pass reveals that the perceived efficiency is purchased by exposing the system more fully to downside conditions. Distribution, redundancy, and alternative channels often look costly in calm periods because their value is not visible in ordinary flow. Concentration removes these seemingly idle supports, creating a cleaner structure. But once removed, the system's response capacity narrows. What has been gained is simplicity. What has been lost is tolerance. The apparent efficiency is therefore not free. It is funded by increased downside sensitivity that remains hidden until tested.

This hidden trade-off explains why concentrated systems can appear strongest just before they are most vulnerable. Calm periods do not test resilience. They reward coherence and uninterrupted flow. A system built for coherence can therefore look exemplary while accumulating structural weakness. When disruption eventually enters, the apparent optimization reveals itself as conditional. The structure was not broadly strong. It was narrowly efficient.

The mechanism resolves into a clear structural principle. Concentration does not increase upside proportionally. It magnifies downside asymmetrically because failure impact becomes concentrated. Narrow support structures may produce calm-condition efficiency, but they also ensure that disruption matters more when it arrives. The system does not become fragile because resources are limited in absolute terms. It becomes fragile because too much continuity depends on too few supports. Income, assets, liquidity, and obligations all become more dangerous when their distribution narrows, because each concentrated point carries more consequence and offers fewer alternatives.

This means stability is inversely related to dependency concentration. As concentration rises, tolerance narrows, substitution weakens, cross-layer fragility intensifies, and downside exposure accelerates. The system may still function smoothly under uninterrupted conditions, but its ability to absorb variance is shrinking beneath that smoothness. When disruption occurs, the cost of narrowness becomes visible all at once. What had seemed efficient proves fragile because the structure was built to work cleanly, not to absorb disturbance broadly.

Systems do not become fragile because resources are limited. They become fragile because too much depends on too little.

The Correlation Mechanism

The Correlation Mechanism begins with a condition that appears stable because its moving parts seem separate. Independence, at the level of observation, is the assumption that variables operate without materially influencing one another. One income stream appears distinct from another. One asset category appears to move on its own. One obligation appears unrelated to another because its timing, label, or surface behavior differs. In calm conditions, this separation is persuasive because the system presents its components as discrete. Their movements are not visibly synchronized, their timing is staggered, and their categories appear unrelated. Independence is therefore first encountered not as a proven structural property but as an observed pattern under low stress.

This distinction matters immediately because observed independence and structural independence are not the same condition. Observed independence means variables appear separate within the environment currently being watched. Structural independence would mean they remain separate even when the environment changes, pressure rises, and latent pathways become active. The first is descriptive and conditional. The second is deeper and more demanding. Calm conditions often reveal only the first. They show that components are not visibly moving together now. They do not establish that no shared dependencies, no hidden constraints, and no common exposure channels exist underneath that current appearance.

At a first level, the illusion of independence is reinforced by differences in timing, category, and presentation. If one variable changes monthly and another changes seasonally, they do not appear linked. If one is labeled as income, another as asset value, and another as expense demand, they appear to belong to separate domains. If one source of strain has historically appeared during one set of conditions and another during a different set, the system treats them as unrelated because their behavior has not visibly overlapped. Surface separation becomes mistaken for structural separation. The eye infers independence from non-simultaneity.

At a deeper level, this inference is conditional on the operating environment remaining calm enough that interaction pathways stay dormant. Low-stress conditions preserve separation because they do not force the system's shared limits into view. Liquidity is sufficient enough that timing differences do not become collisions. Margins are wide enough that one form of pressure does not immediately activate others. Capacity is intact enough that strain in one area does not spread across the structure. Under those conditions, variables can appear independent because the links between them remain inactive. Independence, then, exists as a pattern of observed behavior under specific conditions, not as a permanent guarantee about system structure.

The misinterpretation appears when calm-condition independence is treated as permanent separation. Once that happens, the system begins to model risk as though its components will continue behaving separately even when the environment changes. It assumes that what has not moved together in calm conditions will not move together under strain. This is the central error at the beginning of the mechanism. It does not come from misunderstanding what is visible. It comes from overextending what visibility can prove. The system mistakes present separation for unconditional autonomy.

Stress changes this by activating latent connections. Stress is not simply difficulty or disturbance in a general sense. Structurally, it is the condition under which shared constraints, dependencies, and pathways begin to matter simultaneously. What seemed separate under calm conditions starts moving together because the environment no longer allows inactive linkages to remain dormant. Stress compresses the system. It reduces the distance between variables by forcing them into contact through the shared limits they were always carrying beneath the surface.

At a first level, convergence under stress means that previously separate variables begin to move toward instability at the same time. This does not mean they become identical. It means their behavior becomes aligned in direction and consequence. A strain in one component now coincides with strain in another because both are exposed to the same tightening condition. The system loses the separation that once made each issue appear isolated. Instead of staggered variation, it begins to experience synchronized movement.

This synchronized movement is not created by stress in the sense of being invented out of nothing. Stress reveals it. The shared pathways were already present, but inactive. The calm environment allowed the system to operate without pressing hard enough against common constraints for those pathways to matter. When stress enters, those common constraints are activated. Timing overlap becomes consequential. Shared liquidity dependence becomes visible. Common reliance on the same margin, the same inflow, the same conversion channel, or the same capacity band begins to shape behavior. Correlation is therefore not a new property manufactured at the moment of strain. It is the revealed behavior of a structure whose apparent independence depended on uninterrupted calm.

This is why independence in low-stress conditions differs so sharply from convergence in high-stress conditions. In the first regime, variation can remain unsynchronized because the system has enough room to absorb local disturbance without spreading it. In the second regime, local disturbance reaches shared limits faster, and once those limits are reached, multiple components react together. Stress reduces the system's effective degrees of freedom. It narrows adjustment space, removes timing separation, and makes distinct parts of the structure compete inside the same interval. Convergence is the behavioral result of that compression.

The misinterpretation here is assuming that independence persists across changing system states. That assumption treats calm-state behavior as the governing model for stressed-state behavior. It imagines that the lack of visible alignment under ordinary conditions will survive once pressure activates the system's common exposures. But the operating regime has changed. The system is no longer being observed in the condition that made separation possible. What looked independent was conditional on slack, spacing, and inactive coupling. Once those supports are removed, the observed pattern changes because the real structure becomes more visible than the calm-state appearance ever was.

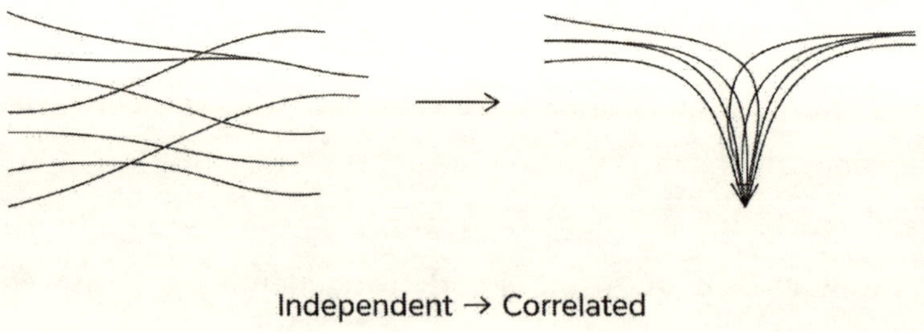

[Figure 5: Correlated Failure Paths]

The breakdown of diversification assumptions follows directly from this shift. Diversification is the distribution of exposure across elements that are assumed not to fail or deteriorate together. Its stabilizing effect depends on non-aligned behavior. If one component weakens while another remains stable, the system can absorb the disturbance because the losses are dispersed. Diversification is therefore not protection by mere plurality. It is protection by separation. The components must remain sufficiently uncorrelated that weakness in one does not immediately imply weakness in the others.

At a first level, diversification appears effective when the system operates in a state where its components are behaving independently. Different inflow sources vary at different times. Different asset forms respond differently to conditions. Different obligations create pressure in staggered sequences. So long as that non-aligned behavior holds, the structure benefits from distribution. The system does not depend on one line, one source, or one moment. Variation is dispersed, and therefore more absorbable.

The mechanism becomes unstable when correlation emerges, because diversification loses its operative basis. Distributed exposure stops functioning as distributed protection once the components begin moving together. If stress causes multiple elements to deteriorate at the same time, then the system is no longer protected by plurality. It is facing synchronized weakness across what had been treated as separate stabilizers. Diversification has not literally disappeared, but its protective logic has. The elements remain numerically distinct while becoming behaviorally aligned.

This shows why diversification is conditional rather than absolute. It reduces risk only while the distributed components retain enough independence to avoid converging under pressure. It is not a permanent shield attached to the mere existence of multiple parts. It is an arrangement whose effectiveness depends on system state. Calm-state diversification can look robust because the conditions necessary for correlation are inactive. Under stress, the hidden common exposures become dominant, and what had looked like multiple separate supports begins acting like one shared failure cluster.

The misinterpretation is treating diversification as protection regardless of system state. This occurs when the system counts the number of components but does not examine whether those components share underlying constraints. It assumes multiplicity alone creates resilience. But distributed components that depend on the same liquidity conditions, the same timing windows, the same operating margins, or the same broad support regime are not structurally separate where it matters most. Their divergence in calm conditions conceals the fact that their failure behavior may still align under stress. Diversification, then, is never stronger than the independence on which it rests.

Once correlation activates, failure pathways begin to align. A failure pathway is the route through which disruption moves from one point into broader instability. Under ordinary conditions, these pathways may activate one at a time, allowing the system to treat disruption as sequential. One issue emerges, adjustment occurs, recovery begins, and only later does another form of pressure arrive. This sequencing matters because it preserves intervals for response. The system does not have to absorb all problems at once. It can move through them in stages.

Correlation changes the structure of failure by synchronizing pathway activation. Multiple pathways begin to carry pressure during the same interval. A timing issue overlaps with an access issue. An inflow disruption coincides with obligation compression. A valuation problem arrives together with liquidity pressure. What had once been separate routes of instability now activate in parallel because the same stress condition is pushing through the system's shared limits. The system no longer encounters one pathway, then another. It encounters several at once.

At a first level, the distinction between sequential and concurrent failure is a distinction between recoverable spacing and compressed stress. Sequential failure allows recovery intervals. One component can weaken without immediately forcing all others into the same state. Concurrent failure removes this advantage. Pressure arrives across multiple components before adjustment, replenishment, or reconfiguration can occur. This is not simply more disruption. It is disruption in a more dangerous form because it denies the system the time structure required for containment.

The structural consequence is that concurrency compresses response capacity. The system may have enough tools to manage one disrupted component at a time, but not several aligned disruptions in the same operating window. Correlation therefore increases the effective size of pressure not just through quantity but through synchronization. The damage lies in how many pathways are active before any one of them can be addressed. The same total amount of stress is more destabilizing when it is simultaneous than when it is spaced.

The misinterpretation is assuming failures will occur independently and sequentially. This assumption is an extension of calm-condition observation into a stress regime where it no longer applies. It imagines that because risks usually appeared one at a time, they will continue to do so even when shared constraints begin binding the system. Once correlation emerges, that model fails. The system does not receive the courtesy of orderly sequencing. Stress activates multiple routes together because the variables were never as separate as they looked.

This leads to the deeper distinction between structural and perceived independence. Perceived independence is separation inferred from surface characteristics. Components look unrelated because they belong to different categories, operate on different schedules, or display different calm-state behavior. Structural independence is more demanding. It requires the absence of shared dependencies, shared constraints, and common pathways that can align behavior under pressure. Surface separation may exist even when underlying coupling remains strong. The crucial question is not whether components look distinct, but whether they are insulated from the same limiting conditions.

At a first level, perceived independence is often built from visibility. One variable is observed in one dashboard, another in another. One belongs to income, another to liquidity, another to obligations, another to assets. Because they are administratively distinct, they are assumed to be structurally distinct. But administrative separation does not prevent common dependence. Different domains can still rely on the same timing precision, the same inflow continuity, the same access channels, or the same capacity margin. Their labels differ while their constraints overlap.

Structural independence requires that these overlaps be absent or weak enough not to matter under pressure. If two components depend on the same liquidity window, they are not structurally independent in stress, even if they appear separate in calm conditions. If several components require the same income continuity, they are linked even if their day-to-day movement differs. If multiple asset forms depend on the same conversion environment to become usable, they share an access constraint even when their nominal values look diverse. Structural linkage is therefore determined by hidden common dependence, not by surface variety.

The misinterpretation arises when independence is evaluated by appearance rather than by system structure. Surface-level difference is mistaken for true separation. This creates a dangerous model because it ignores the pathways that only become visible once the system is strained. Calm conditions reward appearance-based analysis because nothing is forcing hidden connections to reveal themselves. Stress removes that privilege. Once pressure enters, shared constraints become behaviorally decisive, and the difference between perceived and structural independence becomes impossible to ignore.

The structural origin of correlation lies in shared constraints. Correlation does not primarily arise because components resemble each other in abstract form. It arises because they are exposed to the same limiting factors. Shared constraints such as liquidity, timing, dependency channels, and capacity bounds create the common exposures that align system behavior under stress. When a constraint tightens, all components dependent on that constraint begin moving together because they are responding to the same reduction in support.

Liquidity is one of the clearest shared constraints. Multiple components may appear separate until they all require access to usable funds within the same interval. Timing is another. Different obligations, inflows, or conversion processes may seem independent until a compressed schedule forces them into direct conflict. Dependency channels also create shared constraints. Several processes may rely on one inflow source, one access pathway, one operating margin, or one conversion route. Capacity limits unify behavior as well. Components that are otherwise distinct can become correlated simply because they are all drawing from the same finite tolerance.

At a first level, correlation through shared constraints means that disruption to one underlying support condition affects all dependent elements at once. The elements are not aligning because they suddenly became the same. They are aligning because the condition that sustained their apparent independence has weakened. A change in the shared constraint synchronizes their response. This is why correlation is best understood as common exposure behavior. The components are linked through what they depend on, not through how they are labeled.

The misinterpretation is ignoring common dependencies because the visible forms differ. Systems often look for direct similarity and miss indirect shared support. Two components seem diverse because they belong to different categories, but if both depend on the same liquidity reserve or timing precision, then their stress behavior is coupled.

Correlation emerges not from superficial resemblance, but from structural reliance on the same limiting factor. Once that factor becomes active as a constraint, independent drivers give way to shared-constraint drivers.

Time intensifies this mechanism. Stress compresses time for system response, and as time compresses, correlation becomes harder to isolate and more damaging to absorb. Under distributed timing, disruptions can still be handled somewhat independently because there are intervals between them. The system has room to sequence adjustment, restore margin, and prevent one issue from immediately activating another. Under compressed timing, that separation disappears. Multiple pressures arrive inside the same operating window, and once they do, the system loses the temporal structure needed to keep them distinct.

At a first level, time compression reduces the ability to isolate issues. If one problem appears and there is sufficient time before the next, the system can contain it locally. If several problems arrive before any one can be stabilized, the response pathways begin interfering with one another. Resources allocated to one issue are no longer available for another. Recovery intervals vanish. The lack of temporal spacing itself becomes a source of alignment. Problems that might have remained separate in a long interval become correlated because they must now be handled within the same compressed period.

This means correlation increases when adjustment windows shrink. The system no longer experiences pressure as dispersed. It experiences it as stacked. Once recovery time is removed, distinct stresses begin sharing the same consequences because they are all competing for the same limited response capacity at the same moment. Time compression therefore does not merely accompany correlation. It intensifies it by forcing multiple exposures into concurrency.

The misinterpretation is assuming sufficient time always exists to handle disruptions independently. That assumption treats response capacity as if it were governed only by total resources, not by the interval in which those resources must be deployed. But a system can possess adequate total capacity and still fail under compressed timing if several pressures require simultaneous support. Distributed timing allows independence to survive longer. Compressed timing forces alignment by removing recovery intervals between stresses that might otherwise have remained separate.

Feedback loops deepen correlation once it begins. A feedback loop exists when system responses to stress feed back into the conditions that generated the stress. In the context of correlation, this means initial alignment across variables can create new pressure that activates additional linkages, causing even more components to move together. Correlation is therefore not static. It can expand through the system's own reaction.

At a first level, the process begins with initial convergence. Several components weaken together because a shared constraint has tightened. That synchronized weakening increases overall system stress. As total stress rises, margins narrow further, timing becomes more compressed, liquidity becomes more contested, and substitution capacity falls. These changes activate additional common constraints that were previously dormant. Components that had not yet joined the aligned movement are drawn into it because the system has become more compressed.

The recursive structure matters. Initial correlation is not simply observed and then held at that level. The system reacts to the initial alignment, and those reactions intensify the very conditions that create more alignment. A reduction in liquidity support forces additional timing strain. Timing strain then causes more obligations to compete in the same interval. That competition reduces flexibility further, which activates still more shared dependence. Correlation becomes reinforced correlation. The system's responses increase alignment rather than reduce it.

The misinterpretation is treating correlation as a fixed condition rather than as a dynamic process. Under that mistaken model, once some variables become linked, the extent of their linkage is assumed stable. But in stressed systems, correlation can widen as feedback loops activate more of the structure. The first wave of convergence is often only the beginning. What matters is not just that variables moved together, but that moving together increased the conditions that caused them to align in the first place.

The result is non-linear impact. Correlated risks do not merely add to one another. They interact, amplify, and compound because their alignment overwhelms system capacity faster than isolated disturbances would. A system built to absorb one form of pressure at a time may manage several independent disturbances spread across intervals. It may not survive those same disturbances when they align, because the combined demand crosses thresholds that no individual event would have reached alone.

At a first level, additive risk assumes that each disruption can be counted separately and summed without interaction. Correlated risk violates this assumption. Once pressures are aligned, one disruption changes the conditions under which the others are absorbed. Liquidity used for one problem is unavailable for the next. Timing compression created by one delay makes another delay more consequential. A weakened margin in one area lowers tolerance everywhere else. The total impact therefore exceeds simple arithmetic addition because the disruptions are no longer independent inputs. They are interacting within the same constrained system.

This is where threshold crossing becomes decisive. A system may remain stable under isolated stresses because each one stays below the level that would trigger broader instability. Correlated stresses can push the structure across that level even if none of the components would have done so alone. Failure then appears abrupt, but its cause is not a mysteriously large single event. It is combined stress arriving in an aligned form. The system fails because several pressures reach it together and force it across a boundary faster than it can respond.

The misinterpretation is modeling risk as independent and additive. That approach underestimates the consequence of correlation because it assumes total pressure is just the sum of separate parts. But once risks align, the parts interact. They remove each other's buffers, compete for the same capacity, and accelerate one another's effects. Compounding replaces addition. The outcome becomes disproportionate to the apparent size of the initiating stresses.

The governing condition becomes clear once the mechanism is fully developed. Correlation is latent during calm periods because the system has enough spacing, margin, and inactive pathways to allow variables to behave as though they are separate. Stress reveals the underlying alignment by activating shared constraints, compressing time, synchronizing failure pathways, and reinforcing convergence through feedback. Independence is therefore conditional, not permanent. It is a calm-state appearance sustained by untested structure, not a universal description of system behavior.

When stability is tested, correlation becomes the decisive pattern. The system no longer behaves as a collection of isolated components. It behaves as an interconnected structure whose shared constraints determine how pressure moves. Calm-state observation shows what the system looks like when linkages are inactive. Stress shows what the system is when those linkages matter. The relevant behavior for evaluating stability is not the apparent independence of ordinary intervals, but the correlated response that emerges once separation is removed by pressure.

Systems do not behave independently under pressure. Correlation is the governing condition when stability is tested.

The Hidden Coupling Mechanism

The Hidden Coupling Mechanism begins with a structural illusion. Apparent independence masks shared exposure. Components look separate because they are presented separately, managed separately, and often observed separately. Income appears distinct from assets. Assets appear distinct from obligations. Obligations appear distinct from operations. Categories are divided, reporting is segmented, and timing differences reinforce the impression that each part of the system behaves within its own domain. This surface-level independence is real as an observation, but incomplete as an explanation. It describes how the system appears under calm conditions, not how it is actually linked beneath those appearances.

Surface-level independence can be defined as separation inferred from category, timing, or presentation. Two components seem independent when they are labeled differently, move on different schedules, or are administered through different channels. This form of separation is observational. It tells the observer that the components do not obviously collide during ordinary conditions. It does not establish that they are structurally insulated from one another. The distinction is critical because systems can look modular while remaining deeply connected through common pathways that are not visible until pressure activates them.

At a first level, modular appearance is often administrative rather than structural. Income is tracked as inflow. Assets are tracked as stored value. Obligations are tracked as outflow commitments. Operations are tracked as process continuity. Each domain has its own language, reporting interval, and management frame. This segmentation encourages the conclusion that the parts themselves are independent. Yet the separation may exist only at the level of description. The same liquidity window may support assets and obligations. The same income continuity may sustain operations and debt service. The same timing precision may govern access, settlement, and payment execution across what appear to be unrelated categories.

Underlying linkage refers to the shared pathways, dependencies, and constraints that connect these components even when visible interaction is absent. These pathways often remain dormant in calm conditions because the system has enough margin, spacing, and continuity to keep one area's pressure from immediately activating another. As a result, visible separation and hidden linkage can coexist. The system looks segmented because the shared routes are inactive, not because they are absent. Hidden coupling is therefore not a contradiction of surface independence. It is the deeper structural condition that surface observation fails to reveal.

The misinterpretation emerges when category boundaries or presentation formats are treated as proof of independence. This error assumes that because components appear distinct in monitoring and ordinary function, they are insulated in stress behavior as well. But category separation is not the same as structural separation. Administrative distance can coexist with functional dependence. Once that distinction is missed, the system begins to overestimate how much isolation exists between parts that are actually leaning on the same hidden supports.

The structural source of hidden coupling is shared dependency. Components become linked not because they resemble one another in form, but because they rely on the same underlying conditions. Liquidity, timing, income continuity, access channels, and capacity limits are among the most important of these shared supports. When several parts of the system depend on one or more of these conditions, they become structurally connected even if their visible behavior remains separate in calm periods. Hidden coupling is therefore produced by common reliance. It is a property of shared support architecture.

Liquidity is an especially important shared dependency because it often serves multiple roles at once. It bridges timing gaps, absorbs expenses, supports access to obligations, and preserves operating continuity. Assets and obligations may appear unrelated at the surface, yet both can depend on the same liquidity timing. Income and operations may appear distinct, yet both can rely on the same capacity to sustain activity across intervals. What looks like separation by function is often overlap by support. Components that share the same sustaining condition become linked through that condition regardless of whether their ordinary movement appears independent.

This is why dependency overlap creates synchronized vulnerability. If different components rely on the same support base, disruption to that base affects them together. The components do not need to share category, appearance, or ordinary timing behavior to be coupled. They only need to share the same condition of continued support. The coupling lies beneath the visible form. A liquidity constraint can connect assets, obligations, and process continuity. A timing constraint can connect inflows, settlements, and fixed commitments. A capacity constraint can link otherwise separate operations simply because all depend on the same tolerance band.

The distinction here is between independent components and dependency-linked components. Independent components can weaken separately because their support structures are not materially shared. Dependency-linked components only appear independent while their common support remains untested. Once that support tightens, their hidden linkage becomes behaviorally decisive. The failure mode arises when components are evaluated in isolation without mapping the support structures beneath them. This isolates surface behavior while ignoring the common base that will govern their conduct under pressure.

Hidden connections become visible under stress because calm conditions leave many of the system's shared pathways inactive. Latent coupling is not false coupling. It is real structure without present activation. Under low stress, sufficient margin, timing spacing, and support continuity allow linked components to behave as though they are separate. Their underlying connection exists, but it is not transmitting strain. Stress changes this by tightening the constraints that had previously kept the pathways dormant. What was hidden then becomes active.

At a first level, stress reveals hidden coupling by forcing simultaneous strain across components that had appeared unrelated. A timing disruption begins to affect liquidity usage. Liquidity pressure begins to alter asset accessibility. Asset inaccessibility begins to interact with obligations. Operations begin to reflect the strain created elsewhere. These interactions often appear sudden, but their sudden visibility is not the same as sudden creation. The links were already embedded in the structure. Stress merely activates them.

This is why coupling is revealed, not created, by pressure. The system does not invent shared exposure during stress. It discloses it. The calm state concealed the connections because there was enough operating room to prevent strain from moving through them. Once constraints tighten, that room disappears. Hidden pathways convert into active transmission routes. Independence is lost not because the components changed their nature, but because the conditions that preserved their apparent separation have been removed.

The distinction between latent linkage and activated linkage matters because it shifts the explanation from event to structure. A link does not become real only when it is visible. It becomes visible when activation makes it consequential. The failure mode here is believing that connections exist only when they can be observed directly. That belief treats invisibility as absence. In reality, many of the most important system linkages remain invisible precisely because calm conditions do not press hard enough against the structure to reveal them.

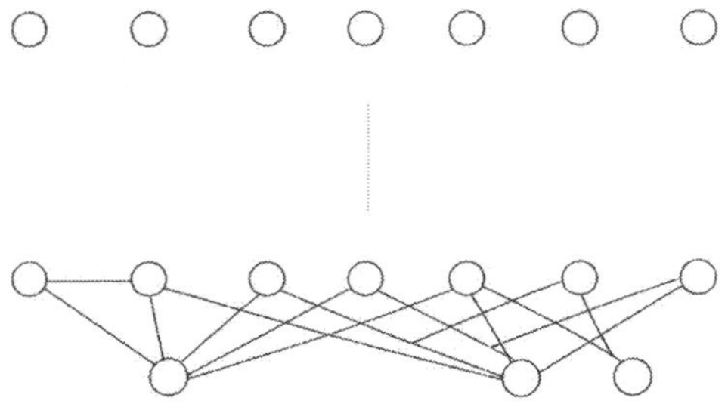

Hidden Connections

[Figure 6: Hidden Coupling Network]

Hidden coupling is not limited to direct connections. Indirect exposure pathways extend linkage beyond obvious relationships. Indirect exposure exists when one component influences another through an intermediate dependency rather than through direct contact. A depends on B, B depends on C, and therefore A depends on C even if no direct relationship between A and C is visible at the surface. This chain-based structure is one of the main reasons systems are more connected than they appear.

At a first level, indirect linkage can be difficult to see because each local relationship looks contained. One component depends on one support. Another depends on another. The overlap only becomes visible when the chain is traced across multiple steps. Calm conditions make this especially difficult because the chain does not need to transmit pressure continuously. Each link can remain quiet while still preserving the possibility of transmission. The absence of visible movement along the chain is then mistaken for the absence of the chain itself.

Mechanistically, indirect pathways allow disturbance to travel farther than expected because each step hands pressure to the next. A strain in access affects liquidity usage. Liquidity usage affects timing flexibility. Timing flexibility affects obligations. Obligations affect operational continuity. The starting point and the end point may appear unrelated if only direct connections are considered. Yet the chain binds them. Systems are therefore connected through networks of stepwise dependence, not only through explicit one-to-one relationships.

The distinction is between direct linkage and indirect linkage. Direct linkage is visible because one component clearly depends on another. Indirect linkage is structurally present but observationally obscure because the dependence runs through intermediate conditions. The failure mode is assuming no connection exists because no direct relationship is visible. This produces a shallow map of the system, one that captures immediate ties while missing the chain-based pathways through which pressure can spread under strain.

Timing creates another form of hidden coupling. Components become linked when their timing requirements converge, even if they differ in substance, category, or function. Under distributed timing, separate components can remain operationally distinct because their demands do not compete inside the same interval. One obligation matures here, one inflow arrives there, one conversion takes place later, and one process completes elsewhere. The spacing itself preserves apparent independence. Stress compresses that spacing.

At a first level, timing alignment links otherwise separate components by forcing them into the same operating window. A resource that could support one demand in one interval may be insufficient when several demands converge at once. Previously separate timelines now compete for the same liquidity, the same settlement period, the same management bandwidth, or the same tolerance margin. This creates coupling through synchronization rather than through resemblance. The components do not need to be structurally similar. They only need to require the same support at the same time.

Compressed timing activates shared dependencies because overlap turns potential competition into actual competition. An access delay that would have been manageable in a wider interval becomes destabilizing when it overlaps with clustered obligations. An inflow that would have sustained operations under normal spacing becomes insufficient when several outflows converge before replenishment. Timing therefore creates functional dependence. Separate elements become linked because their survival now depends on the same narrow window being sufficient for all of them.

The distinction here is between distributed timing and aligned timing. Distributed timing preserves separation by spacing pressure. Aligned timing removes that spacing and forces multiple components into direct interaction. The failure mode lies in ignoring timing overlap as a source of structural linkage. Systems often recognize shared resources but overlook shared intervals. Yet timing can create coupling even when no direct common asset, common category, or visible common structure seems present. Synchronization itself becomes the link.

When multiple couplings overlap, the system moves from partial linkage into entanglement. Entanglement is a condition of dense interconnection across many pathways at once. It exists when multiple shared dependencies, indirect chains, timing alignments, and common support structures overlap so extensively that components lose meaningful isolation. The system can no longer be understood as a set of independent parts with occasional contact. It behaves as a network whose nodes transmit pressure across many routes simultaneously.

At a first level, entanglement means that several couplings are active together. A liquidity constraint interacts with a timing constraint. A timing constraint interacts with operational sequencing. Operational strain interacts with obligation pressure. Each coupling reinforces the effects of the others. The result is not just more linkage, but a change in system behavior. Local stress stops remaining local because every affected node is connected to other stressed nodes through multiple routes rather than one.

This is what distinguishes partial coupling from full entanglement. In partial coupling, one or two relationships may transmit strain while the rest of the structure remains comparatively insulated. In entangled systems, multiple pathways overlap to such an extent that stress can move broadly without needing a single dominant channel. The system's components lose isolation entirely in functional terms. One area's pressure becomes relevant to many others at once because the network of linkages is dense enough to distribute disturbance rapidly.

The failure mode is treating connections as isolated instead of networked. If each coupling is examined separately, the overall density of interconnection is missed. The system can then appear safer than it is because the analysis recognizes individual links but not the fact that many links overlap on the same nodes and intervals. Entanglement is therefore not simply a larger number of connections. It is the condition in which overlapping connections change the system's mode of behavior from segmented to unified under stress.

Coupling density determines how quickly and how broadly pressure can travel. Coupling density is the number and strength of the connections linking system components. Sparse coupling means fewer and weaker pathways, which preserve isolation and allow more local damping. Dense coupling means more numerous and stronger pathways, which reduce the system's ability to keep pressure contained. As density rises, propagation potential rises with it. The system becomes more sensitive because stress has more ways to move.

At a first level, dense coupling lowers isolation capacity. If one component weakens, there are many routes through which that weakness can affect others. The problem is not only the existence of connection, but the cumulative effect of many connections operating at once. A sparse system may still transmit disruption, but the routes are fewer, slower, and easier to interrupt. A dense system transmits quickly because there are multiple overlapping channels available for strain to follow.

This changes the balance between damping and transmission. Sparse coupling preserves damping because local pressure can dissipate before finding many downstream routes. Dense coupling weakens damping because the pressure encounters connected nodes before local absorption can finish. The system has less time, less separation, and fewer boundaries between disturbance and broad consequence. More connection does not necessarily produce more resilience. It often produces greater propagation risk because it increases the number of available transmission paths.

The distinction is therefore between sparse coupling and dense coupling. Sparse systems can preserve local variation without immediate system-wide consequence. Dense systems convert local variation into network pressure more readily. The failure mode is assuming that more connection automatically improves resilience because it seems to increase integration. Integration can improve flow in calm periods while worsening propagation under stress. What appears well-connected may in fact be highly transmissive.

Hidden coupling also leads systems to misprice their own stability. Calm periods conceal coupling because inactive pathways do not generate visible signals. Components appear independent because nothing has yet forced simultaneous strain through their shared supports. The absence of concurrent stress then reinforces the belief that separation is real and durable. Stability is measured by calm-state performance, and calm-state performance looks strong precisely because the pathways that would reveal fragility remain dormant.

At a first level, this produces false confidence in diversification and separation. If income, assets, obligations, and operations have not visibly collided, the system infers that they are effectively insulated. If one source of pressure has not historically activated another, the system treats them as independent. This is a pricing error in structural terms. The system assigns low significance to linkages that have not yet been behaviorally tested, even when those linkages are already embedded beneath the surface.

The deeper problem is that perceived stability can increase as actual coupling increases. Repeated calm cycles encourage further integration, tighter synchronization, and greater dependence on shared supports. Because nothing breaks, these moves are interpreted as improvements in efficiency or coherence. Yet each added connection can increase shared exposure. The system therefore becomes more coupled while also becoming more confident. Fragility grows without visible warning because the same calm that validates the structure also conceals the pathways through which it would fail.

The distinction here is between perceived resilience and actual structural exposure. Perceived resilience is derived from calm-state observation. Actual exposure is determined by the density and invisibility of the connections that will activate under stress. The failure mode lies in using calm-state performance as proof of structural independence. That proof is invalid because the operating regime that preserved separation is the same regime that prevented hidden coupling from becoming visible.

Once hidden coupling activates, cascade becomes possible. A cascade is the propagation of disruption across multiple components through the system's pre-existing connection structure. Hidden coupling makes cascade more dangerous because it allows rapid spread through routes that were not being actively monitored as transmission channels during calm periods. When stress activates both direct and indirect linkages, the system discovers that many more components are reachable from the point of origin than it had assumed.

At a first level, cascade is the difference between local disruption and network consequence. A problem begins in one node, but does not stop there. Direct linkages transmit pressure immediately. Indirect linkages extend it through intermediate dependencies. Timing alignment forces multiple demands into the same interval. Shared supports weaken across several domains at once. The spread is not random. It follows the architecture that was already present. Hidden coupling determines both the reach and the speed of that spread.

This is why cascades are structural rather than accidental. They do not happen because many unrelated failures coincidentally arrive together. They happen because the system was already wired in a way that allowed one form of strain to activate many others. Direct and indirect couplings combine during failure, making the total network response much broader than the initiating event. The reach of the cascade depends on how many components share the same supports, the same timing pressures, or the same chain-based dependencies.

The distinction is between local disruption and network cascade. A truly isolated component can fail locally. A hiddenly coupled network cannot rely on local containment once activation begins. The failure mode is treating disruptions as isolated when the structure makes them transmissible. That assumption is especially dangerous because it ignores the very routes that matter most once the system is stressed.

The structural resolution of the mechanism follows from all of this. Apparent independence masks shared exposure. Systems that look divided into separate categories are often joined underneath by common dependencies, indirect pathways, synchronized timing, overlapping supports, and dense coupling networks. Calm conditions conceal these linkages because the system has enough operating room to keep them inactive. Stress reveals them by tightening constraints and forcing the structure to behave according to its underlying connectivity rather than its surface presentation.

Coupling governs system behavior under stress because it determines how pressure moves, how fast local problems become shared problems, and how many components are affected before recovery can occur. As linkage becomes denser and less visible, systemic risk rises. The danger does not come from overt concentration alone. It comes from hidden interdependence embedded inside structures that appear modular. What looks like separation at the surface becomes shared vulnerability once strain activates the common support architecture beneath it.

Systems are not collections of independent parts. They are networks of shared exposure revealed under pressure.

The Threshold Breach Mechanism

The Threshold Breach Mechanism begins with a structural fact that is often obscured by calm conditions: systems operate within boundaries, not in open-ended continuity. A threshold is a structural boundary within which the system can absorb variation, maintain continuity, and preserve its operating logic without entering instability. It is not a symbolic line or a theoretical abstraction. It is an embedded property of configuration. The threshold exists wherever the system's liquidity, timing precision, dependency structure, and tolerance margin define the limit of what can be sustained without a change in state. The system can function on either side of that limit, but it does not function according to the same rules in both regimes.

This makes it necessary to distinguish between operating range and failure boundary. The operating range is the zone within which pressure, variation, and disturbance remain absorbable. Inside that range, the system can experience strain without losing structural continuity. The failure boundary is the point beyond which those same mechanisms no longer preserve order. Once crossed, the system does not merely become somewhat weaker. It enters a different regime of behavior in which prior adjustment methods lose effectiveness and accumulated pressure begins expressing itself as visible instability. A threshold, then, is not a vague edge to comfort. It is the point at which structural absorbency gives way to structural breakdown.

Limits are the specific forms in which thresholds are embedded. Liquidity limits define how much timing disruption or expense pressure can be absorbed before operational continuity fails. Timing limits define how much sequence compression can occur before obligations begin colliding faster than they can be resolved. Dependency limits define how much reliance can be placed on narrow channels before interruption becomes system-threatening. Structural tolerance limits define how much combined stress the full arrangement can carry before its internal relationships stop dampening and begin transmitting pressure. These limits are continuous conditions. They do not appear only when they are approached. They exist at all times because they are built into the system's architecture.

The crucial distinction is between threshold presence and threshold awareness. A system can be governed by strict thresholds without recognizing how near it is to them. Awareness is observational and often incomplete. Presence is structural and constant. This distinction matters because the system's behavior is governed by the thresholds that exist, not by the thresholds it has correctly identified. The incorrect interpretation treats limits as distant or theoretical, as though they become relevant only in extreme scenarios. That interpretation mistakes calm operating conditions for evidence that boundaries are remote. In reality, calm operation does not move the threshold. It merely means the system is presently functioning within it.

Stability, therefore, is not the absence of pressure. It is the condition of operating inside bounds. Within those bounds, the system absorbs variation without structural consequence. An expense can rise. Timing can tighten modestly. Access can become slightly slower. One dependency can weaken without immediate collapse. The reason these movements do not produce overt instability is not that they are trivial in themselves, but that they remain within the tolerance band that the system can still manage. Stability under such conditions is often misread as intrinsic strength. More precisely, it is bounded stability. It exists because the system has not yet crossed the point at which its dampening mechanisms cease to function adequately.

Within the operating range, variation remains containable. Localized strain can be offset by liquidity, by timing flexibility, by partial substitution, by temporary compression that does not yet destroy continuity, or by small internal redistributions that preserve the overall structure. These responses can be costly, but they remain structurally normal. The system is still processing pressure using its native operating logic. This is what makes the stable zone so difficult to interpret correctly. Because strain can be absorbed there, the system appears robust. But what appears as robustness may simply be operation inside tolerable bounds.

Beyond thresholds, the behavior changes. Normal adjustment mechanisms stop working in their prior form because the system has moved past the conditions under which they were sufficient. Liquidity is no longer buffering timing mismatch; it is being exhausted by it. Flexibility is no longer absorbing obligation pressure; it is disappearing under it. Dependencies are no longer manageable concentrations; they are becoming failure channels. Once beyond the threshold, the system does not experience more of the same pressure at a larger magnitude. It experiences a change in state. This is the key distinction between absorption and structural breakdown. One belongs to bounded operation. The other belongs to post-boundary behavior.

This means stability must be understood as conditional. It depends on remaining within the range where pressure can be absorbed without changing the rules by which the system operates. The absence of visible breakdown is not proof that the system is strong in an unqualified sense. It is proof only that pressure has not yet forced the structure beyond its active boundaries. The incorrect interpretation assumes that because the system has handled prior strain, it will continue doing so proportionally as strain increases. That assumption fails because thresholds divide system behavior into regimes. Conditions that are manageable inside the range can become destabilizing once the boundary is crossed, even if the increment of additional stress is small.

The transition from stable to unstable is therefore nonlinear. Threshold crossing does not produce gradual decline according to a simple linear scale. It produces discontinuity. Small additional stress near the boundary can generate disproportionately large outcomes because the system is no longer operating under the same response structure as before. The key error in linear interpretation is assuming that each additional unit of pressure has roughly the same consequence regardless of where the system stands relative to its limits. But consequence is not evenly distributed across the range. Near the threshold, the system's remaining margin has become thin enough that one more increment of pressure can trigger state change.

This discontinuity can be described as a transition from one regime to another. In the stable regime, pressure is processed through absorption. In the unstable regime, pressure is processed through propagation, depletion, and breakdown. The same type of stress can behave differently depending on which side of the threshold the system occupies. A timing delay that is manageable when liquidity remains intact becomes destabilizing when liquidity is already compressed. A concentrated expense that is absorbable with available margin becomes catastrophic when margin has already been consumed by prior strain. Behavior on either side of the threshold follows different rules because the system's internal capacity to dampen disturbance is no longer the same.

The incorrect interpretation assumes stress impact scales proportionally across all ranges. Under that view, if a certain level of pressure produced modest difficulty before, a slightly higher level should produce slightly greater difficulty now. This logic fails at thresholds. The additional stress near a boundary does not simply add burden. It activates a different response mode. That is why small marginal changes can appear to cause implausibly large outcomes. The large outcome is not caused by the small increment alone. It is caused by the fact that the increment arrived at the point where the prior operating regime could no longer hold.

This explains why systems can remain apparently normal while moving much closer to failure. Proximity to the threshold is not directly visible in calm conditions. A system can approach the boundary without obvious warning because the visible state may still look stable while the margin that supports that appearance is steadily compressing. The operating surface remains smooth precisely because the system continues functioning inside the boundary, even if only narrowly. As long as the threshold has not yet been crossed, the appearance of order can persist. This creates latent proximity: the system is near failure while still looking normal.

Visible stability and latent proximity are therefore distinct conditions. The first is what can be observed at the surface. The second describes the shrinking distance between current operating pressure and the point of instability. Margin compression is the main reason this becomes hard to perceive. A system may still be meeting obligations, still converting assets when needed, still absorbing expense variation, and still maintaining process continuity. Yet each of these may be occurring with less slack, more timing precision, and greater dependence on uninterrupted support. The structure is moving closer to the threshold even though its outward behavior has not yet changed regime.

This hidden proximity is one of the most consequential properties of thresholds. Risk increases before any visible sign of instability appears. That increase is structural, not emotional or interpretive. The system's distance to failure has shortened, even if no failure signal is present. The incorrect interpretation treats visible calm as evidence that failure remains remote. But threshold distance cannot be read directly from surface performance. A system can look identical at two points in time while carrying radically different remaining tolerance because the invisible buffer separating ordinary function from instability has narrowed. Calm appearance therefore cannot be used as a reliable measure of safety.

Once the threshold is breached, breakdown behavior appears sudden. The system moves quickly from apparent continuity into visible disorder because the transition was nonlinear. The accumulation phase that brought the structure near the boundary was often gradual, but its effects remained largely latent. The activation phase begins only when the boundary is crossed. At that point, accumulated pressure that had been compressed into hidden vulnerability becomes visible as breakdown. This is why failure often looks abrupt. The visibility of failure begins late in the process, even though the structural deterioration that enabled it began earlier.

It is necessary here to distinguish between accumulation phase and activation phase. During accumulation, pressure builds, margins compress, dependency sensitivity rises, and distance to the threshold narrows. Yet the system remains inside the stable zone, so the effects are muted, delayed, or absorbed. During activation, those previously accumulated conditions begin expressing themselves visibly because the system has moved into the instability regime. The failure seems sudden because the visible consequences are concentrated at the breach point. The structural process, however, was not sudden. It was the long compression of tolerance beneath an unchanged outward surface.

Suddenness is therefore a perception artifact, not a structural reality. The system did not move from healthy to unstable without intermediate development. It moved through a phase in which risk was accumulating faster than visible symptoms were appearing. The incorrect interpretation reads the final transition as abrupt and unpredictable because it focuses on the visibility of breakdown rather than on the existence of an invisible threshold process. But threshold-driven failure is not random. It is the moment when conditions that had been structurally worsening finally cross the line beyond which the prior regime can no longer sustain itself.

Thresholds do not operate in isolation from the rest of the system's architecture. They are shaped and repositioned by the other mechanisms already embedded in the structure. Concentration lowers thresholds because narrow dependency channels reduce the amount of disruption the system can absorb before continuity breaks. When too much depends on too little, each affected input carries more consequence, so the operating range shrinks. Correlation pushes multiple variables toward thresholds simultaneously. What looked like independent pressures begin aligning, and several boundaries may be approached at once rather than sequentially. Hidden coupling activates multiple thresholds in connected domains because shared exposure routes allow strain to travel from one component into others that were thought to be separate. Expense shocks accelerate approach to the boundary by compressing time, drawing down liquidity, and forcing several demands into the same interval.

This means the relevant distinction is between independent limits and interacting limits. An independent-limit interpretation would treat each boundary as a separate issue: a liquidity threshold here, a timing threshold there, an obligation threshold elsewhere. But in actual structural operation, these limits interact. Margin lost in one area lowers effective tolerance in another. Timing compression increases liquidity sensitivity. Dependency concentration amplifies the impact of an expense shock. Correlated strain removes sequential recovery intervals, forcing several thresholds into the same operating window. The system is therefore governed not by isolated boundaries but by a network of mutually influencing limits.

This interaction changes how breach occurs. The system may not cross one threshold cleanly while all others remain undisturbed. Instead, one near-breach condition can pull other limits closer through shared dependencies and feedback. A liquidity drawdown may reduce timing flexibility. Reduced timing flexibility may increase obligation pressure. Obligation pressure may force asset access under unfavorable conditions. Each step lowers tolerance elsewhere. Thresholds, then, are not merely endpoints waiting independently to be reached. They are dynamic boundary conditions shaped by the current state of the whole structure.

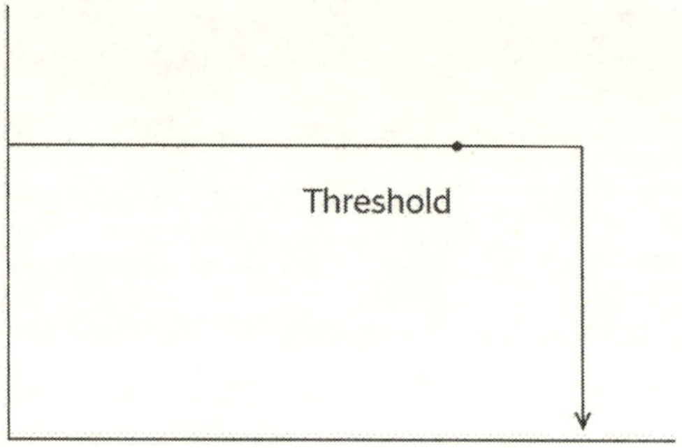

[Figure 7: Threshold Breach Curve]

The threshold breach curve makes this visible. Along the horizontal axis, system stress or load increases. Along the vertical axis, system stability remains high across the stable zone while stress remains within absorbable bounds. The curve then reaches an inflection point at the threshold boundary. Beyond that point, stability declines rapidly. The sharp change does not imply that the system was unaffected by rising stress beforehand. It implies that the effects of rising stress remained largely absorbed until the limit of absorbency was crossed. The instability zone begins where the operating rules change. What had been gradual compression becomes rapid decline because the system is no longer processing stress inside its previous tolerance band.

This visual form matters because it clarifies that the threshold is not a symbolic midpoint but a regime divider. The stable zone can contain considerable stress without visible breakdown. The threshold boundary marks the point where further stress no longer produces incremental cost alone, but state change. The instability zone then reflects a different structural logic: propagation overwhelms damping, accumulated pressure becomes visible, and decline accelerates because the system is now operating beyond its capacity to remain organized under load.

Risk accumulation before activation is one of the central implications of this mechanism. Systems can carry increasing stress without triggering breakdown because accumulation and failure are not the same event. Accumulated risk is the structural compression of margin, flexibility, and tolerance that occurs before the threshold is crossed. Realized failure is the activation of that compression into visible instability. The distinction matters because it prevents the false conclusion that no failure means no increasing danger. A system can be carrying substantial latent instability while still performing its ordinary functions.

This accumulation phase is structurally real but observationally quiet. Pressure builds through concentration, through narrowing timing windows, through growing dependence on uninterrupted inflow, through increased asset inaccessibility under stress, through rising obligation density, and through hidden coupling across components. Each of these developments can increase total vulnerability without immediately activating collapse. The system remains in the stable regime, so the accumulated strain remains partly masked. Calm observation therefore sees continuity where structural analysis sees diminishing distance to boundary.

The breach does not create this accumulated pressure. It activates it. This is the distinction between accumulated risk and realized failure. The origin of instability lies in the earlier build-up of conditions that reduced the distance to the threshold. The breach is the moment those conditions cease to remain latent. Because visibility begins at activation, the system may misread failure as having begun at the breach point. In reality, the breach is the point at which prior instability becomes legible. It is not the point at which vulnerability first came into existence.

This resolves the mechanism. Systems do not fail because pressure suddenly appears. They fail because accumulated pressure crosses a structural boundary. Stability can persist while risk increases because the system may still be operating inside its threshold even as its margin narrows. Failure occurs when limits are exceeded, not when stress begins. The decisive feature of the system is not whether stress is present, since stress is often continuously present in some degree, but whether the structure remains within the range where it can still absorb that stress without changing state.

The final principle follows directly. Systems are governed by thresholds that remain invisible until crossed. Failure is not the beginning of instability. It is the moment accumulated instability becomes visible.

The Cascade Mechanism

The Cascade Mechanism defines failure as a transmitted process rather than an isolated event. Cascade occurs when disruption entering one part of a system moves through pre-existing connections into additional components, producing an ordered progression from local disturbance to broader instability. It is not simultaneous collapse across all areas at once. It is sequential failure propagation. One component weakens, the effects travel, downstream functions absorb the disturbance imperfectly, and the resulting pressure continues outward. The defining characteristic is not mere multiplicity of failures, but structured transmission. Failure spreads because the system contains pathways through which disturbance can move.

This distinction separates isolated failure from propagated failure. An isolated failure remains bounded to the component in which it begins. It may impose cost, but it does not alter the operating state of the larger structure. A propagated failure does not remain local. Its initial disturbance enters one node, but the node's dependencies, timing relationships, and shared resource conditions allow the disruption to travel. The sequence matters. Cascade is not a collection of unrelated problems arriving near one another in time. It is an ordered process in which one strain becomes the condition for the next. The incorrect interpretation treats cascading events as coincidental or separate failures merely because their visible manifestations appear in different domains. That interpretation misses the structural continuity linking them.

A cascade therefore follows pre-existing pathways rather than forming randomly. The system does not improvise routes for failure at the moment of stress. Those routes already exist in dependency chains, timing sequences, liquidity flows, access conditions, and operating constraints. What the triggering event does is activate them. This makes cascade a structural property of connected systems, not a descriptive label for episodes that happen to end badly. When disruption moves in sequence from one zone to another, the important question is not why many things failed near the same time, but through which existing linkages one failure became several.

The initial trigger must be distinguished from the system response it produces. The trigger is the first disturbance entering the structure. It may be a delayed inflow, an unexpected expense, a blocked access channel, a valuation shock, a process interruption, or any other event that introduces pressure into one point of operation. But the trigger alone does not determine the size or reach of the ultimate outcome. Its significance depends on what kind of structure receives it. A system with segmentation, margin, and alternative pathways can absorb the same trigger that would destabilize a tightly connected structure. The trigger initiates. The structure determines what follows.

This distinction is essential because outcome is often misattributed to event magnitude alone. A modest disturbance may produce severe system-wide damage in one structure while a larger disturbance remains contained in another. The difference lies in structural sensitivity. Sensitivity is determined by how close the system is to its thresholds, how concentrated its dependencies are, how narrow its adjustment paths have become, and how many couplings connect the affected component to others. Identical triggers therefore do not produce identical consequences. The system response is governed by configuration, not by event size in isolation.

A structural reading of failure shifts explanation away from the initiating event and toward the way the system receives and transmits it. When a small interruption becomes a large breakdown, the large breakdown is not evidence that the small interruption was somehow secretly large. It is evidence that the system had a high transmission capacity for disturbance. The incorrect interpretation focuses on the trigger because it is easiest to identify. The correct interpretation locates explanatory weight in the response architecture. Once cascade is active, later stages often matter more than the originating event because the structure expands the disturbance as it moves.

Interconnected systems are especially vulnerable to this progression because they do not permit components to fail independently once cascade begins. Interconnection means that multiple functions rely on shared resources, common sequences, or overlapping support conditions. A local strain therefore does not remain a local variable. It enters a field of connected components that all depend, directly or indirectly, on the same sustaining pathways. Once cascade starts, the idea of independent component failure becomes increasingly inaccurate. The system behaves as a connected structure whose parts are transmitting stress to one another.

This is where the distinction between segmented systems and interconnected systems becomes decisive. In segmented systems, boundaries slow or halt the movement of disruption. One component can weaken without automatically compromising all adjacent functions because the structure preserves local isolation. In interconnected systems, that isolation is reduced. Dependencies overlap, resource channels are shared, and timing connections align functions that seemed separate under calm conditions. Breakdown then emerges not from one component's weakness alone, but from the density of the links through which that weakness can travel.

Dependency chains are one of the clearest expressions of this. If one function depends on another, and that second function depends on a third, then pressure entering the chain can move across all of them even if only the first visibly failed at the outset. Shared resources create similar transmission. Components drawing on the same liquidity, access capacity, operational bandwidth, or timing margin become linked because depletion or disruption in one area alters the conditions available to the rest. Timing connections intensify this by forcing multiple dependencies into the same interval, narrowing adjustment space. Interconnected breakdown is therefore not an accumulation of independent failures, but the unfolding of one transmitted process across a linked structure.

The pathways of propagation determine how cascade moves. A pathway is not simply any connection. It is a route through which pressure is carried forward with structural consequence. Dependency chains form one class of pathway. If one node supports several downstream functions, its weakening becomes a transport mechanism for strain. Timing sequences form another. If one event must occur before another remains feasible, delay or failure at the start of the sequence propagates pressure through all subsequent stages. Resource flows constitute another path. Liquidity, access, and usable capacity move through systems according to structured routes, and a disruption in those routes can redirect, compress, or starve functions downstream.

Each pathway determines direction, speed, and reach. Direction matters because not every link carries pressure the same way. Some nodes are upstream of many others, some are downstream, and some are central transfer points. Speed matters because tight coupling allows disturbance to move rapidly, reducing the time available for local adjustment. Reach matters because some pathways terminate locally while others extend across multiple domains. The system's cascade behavior is therefore path-dependent. Failure does not simply spread everywhere equally. It travels according to the connection geometry already embedded in the structure.

This distinguishes direct transmission from pathway-driven propagation. Direct transmission is the immediate movement of strain from one component to another visibly connected one. Pathway-driven propagation includes the longer, structured routes by which failure moves through intermediate dependencies, sequential timing demands, and shared support channels. The incorrect interpretation tends to notice only the direct links because they are easier to see. But many of the most important cascade effects occur through multi-step routes that remain partly hidden until the system is under stress. A pathway analysis therefore explains not only that failure spread, but how and why it reached the places it did.

The cascade itself unfolds in three stages: trigger, propagation, and amplification. The trigger is the initial disturbance. Propagation is the movement of that disturbance through the system's pathways. Amplification is the increase in consequence that occurs as the transmitted pressure interacts with structural weaknesses downstream. These stages must be separated because the event origin does not explain the full outcome. Once propagation begins, the system starts converting local disturbance into broader pressure. Once amplification begins, the transmitted disturbance becomes larger in effect than the initiating event would suggest.

The trigger phase is often the most visible at the start because it is the first identifiable point of disruption. But propagation is where the system reveals its connection logic. The disturbance begins to alter timing elsewhere, constrain resource availability elsewhere, or activate dependencies that had not yet been under visible stress. Amplification then emerges when those newly affected areas are themselves low-margin, tightly coupled, or concentration-heavy. The cascade is no longer just moving. It is growing.

This distinction between event origin and cascade evolution matters because later stages frequently dominate the outcome. A trigger may be moderate, but if propagation reaches sensitive nodes and amplification begins, the final consequence can be severe. The system's collapse pattern is therefore often explained more by what happened after the initial event than by the initiating event itself. The incorrect interpretation compresses all causal weight into the origin. A structural reading follows the disturbance across stages and recognizes that the system, not the trigger, produces much of the final scale.

Amplification depends on structural weakness. Transmission alone does not guarantee collapse. A disturbance can move through a system and still remain manageable if the components receiving it have sufficient damping capacity. Collapse becomes more likely when propagation enters weak links, tightly coupled areas, or zones without buffering. These structural weaknesses increase cascade intensity because they do not merely pass the disturbance along. They enlarge its effects. Chapter 8 established that weakness is the tendency to amplify disturbance rather than absorb it. Cascade converts that insight into sequence. As transmitted strain reaches weak structure, local pressure becomes multiplied pressure.

Weak links matter because they set the points at which transmitted stress ceases to remain manageable. Tight coupling matters because it reduces delay between one stage of propagation and the next. Lack of buffering matters because it removes the reserves and spacing that might otherwise dampen the disturbance before it expands. Amplification is therefore not produced by the event itself. It is produced by the interaction between propagated pressure and the receiving structure's inability to contain or absorb it. This is the distinction between transmission and multiplication. A system may carry failure forward without greatly enlarging it, or it may convert modest incoming strain into disproportionate downstream damage.

Feedback loops intensify this further by turning linear propagation into recursive amplification. In linear propagation, disturbance moves one direction through the structure: node to node, sequence to sequence, domain to domain. In feedback-driven escalation, the system's own reaction to the disturbance creates new stress that re-enters the network and worsens the original conditions. The initial failure alters the state of the system, and that altered state increases the force of later propagation. Collapse becomes self-reinforcing.

This recursive behavior can take many structural forms. A liquidity disruption forces compressed timing, which then increases obligation pressure, which then accelerates further liquidity stress. An operational interruption delays one sequence, which creates congestion elsewhere, which then feeds back into the original bottleneck. An access problem forces asset conversion under adverse timing, which weakens reserves, which then intensifies later access fragility. In each case, system response increases system stress. Cascade is no longer a one-time chain moving outward. It becomes a loop in which each stage worsens the conditions for the next.

The incorrect interpretation treats cascade as a one-directional chain that simply runs its course. That view underestimates how much the system itself can participate in its own destabilization once feedback is active. Recursive amplification changes the tempo of collapse. What had been an ordered sequence becomes a self-accelerating one because the outputs of one failure stage become inputs into the next round of stress. The distinction, then, is between one-directional propagation and feedback-driven escalation. The former spreads disturbance. The latter grows it through repetition.

Cascade also crosses domains. Failure does not remain confined to its origin domain because domain boundaries are not structural barriers when shared dependencies and hidden couplings connect them. Income disruption can propagate into liquidity pressure. Liquidity pressure can propagate into obligations. Obligation strain can affect operations. Operational weakness can force asset access or liquidation. Asset disruption can then feed back into liquidity and future income stability. The point is not that every cascade must follow this exact order. It is that once inter-domain linkages exist, local domain failure can spill into adjacent domains through the supports they share.

This is the distinction between domain-local failure and cross-domain cascade. A failure remains domain-local only if the structure prevents its conditions from becoming relevant elsewhere. In interconnected systems, that prevention is often weak. Shared dependencies mean that one domain's pressure quickly changes the resource, timing, or access conditions on which another depends. Cross-domain spillover is therefore not unusual or exceptional. It is a predictable consequence of shared support architecture.

The system often misreads domain boundaries as if they were containment boundaries. Income, liquidity, operations, obligations, and assets are administratively distinct. But administrative distinction does not prevent propagation when support conditions overlap. A delayed inflow is not "just an income issue" if liquidity bridging depends on it. A liquidity shortfall is not "just a cash issue" if obligations and operations are timed around that cash's availability. Spillover occurs because shared support makes domains permeable. Once cascade begins, the domain in which failure started loses explanatory priority relative to the connections through which it travels.

Containment fails when the structure lacks the capacity to absorb disruption locally and stop its movement outward. Containment capacity is the system's ability to preserve local boundaries under stress. It depends on buffers, segmentation, redundancy, and sufficient margins. Without these, pressure bypasses local defenses and continues into adjacent functions. The difference between contained disruption and uncontained cascade is therefore not the presence of stress, but the presence of structural limits on transmission.

Buffers matter because they absorb pressure without requiring immediate transfer. Segmentation matters because it reduces the number of channels through which local failure can spread. Redundancy matters because alternate pathways allow function to continue without overloading the damaged route. Margins matter because they preserve tolerance during early propagation stages. When these conditions are absent or weak, containment fails. The system does not have enough structural resistance to keep disturbance in place.

This failure of containment is often mistaken for event severity rather than structural insufficiency. But the same trigger in a better-segmented, more buffered, less concentrated system may never have become a cascade. The correct analysis asks why local boundaries failed to hold. It does not stop at the observation that they failed. Containment capacity is therefore one of the central differentiators between structures that suffer isolated disruption and structures that enter uncontained cascade.

Cascade often appears to culminate in sudden collapse, but this appearance is misleading. The actual propagation timeline is sequential and continuous. The reason collapse looks sudden is that earlier stages remain partially hidden while later stages activate visible system-wide effects. During early propagation, pressure may still be moving through pathways without having yet produced broad observable disorder. By the time multiple domains are visibly affected, the underlying sequence has often been running for some time. Observation starts late relative to structure.

This creates the distinction between observed collapse and actual propagation timeline. Observed collapse refers to the point at which the disturbance becomes undeniable at the surface. The actual propagation timeline includes the earlier trigger phase, the initial pathway activation, the first instances of local amplification, and the early cross-domain spillovers that may not yet have been recognized as parts of one process. Suddenness is therefore a perception artifact produced by delayed visibility. The cascade was not sudden. The recognition of it was.

This distinction matters because it prevents misclassification of failure as abrupt or unpredictable when it was actually threshold-driven and pathway-mediated. If earlier stages remain partly hidden, later visible stages will look explosive. But the explosion is often the result of accumulated propagation finally reaching domains where its consequences can no longer remain obscured. The system did not jump from stability to collapse without intermediate development. It transmitted, amplified, fed back, and spilled over before the collapse became fully legible.

Cascade is also best understood as the expression of combined prior mechanisms. The Single Point of Failure Mechanism often provides the origin of cascade by concentrating too much continuity into one node. The Concentration Mechanism increases cascade impact by ensuring that disruption to a few inputs carries disproportionate consequences. The Correlation Mechanism synchronizes multiple cascades or multiple pressure channels, compressing response intervals and making parallel propagation more likely. The Hidden Coupling Mechanism expands propagation pathways by revealing the shared exposures and indirect routes through which disturbance can travel. The Threshold Breach Mechanism activates cascade state by moving the system beyond the regime in which local absorption remains sufficient.

This means the distinction is not between standalone failure and system-level cascade in merely descriptive terms. Standalone failure is what the system appears to have when only the origin is examined. System-level cascade is what the system actually has when the combined mechanisms are traced across the full structure. Cascade is the dynamic expression of prior vulnerabilities becoming active together. It is not a separate category standing outside the earlier mechanisms. It is what those mechanisms produce once transmission begins.

The structural conditions for cascade are therefore identifiable in advance, even if the specific trigger is not. High coupling creates abundant transmission routes. Low redundancy removes alternate pathways and binary failure conditions become more likely. Compressed margins shorten the distance from local strain to threshold breach. Aligned timing pressures reduce recovery intervals and force multiple stresses into the same window. These conditions do not guarantee cascade on every occasion, but they define cascade potential. A system may contain the potential for cascade long before that potential is activated.

This clarifies the distinction between cascade potential and cascade activation. Potential refers to the structure's built-in capacity to transmit and amplify failure. Activation occurs when a trigger enters and the structure begins behaving according to that capacity. Systems are not equally vulnerable by chance. They are cascade-prone or cascade-resistant according to design. The trigger determines when the mechanism begins operating. The structure determines whether it can operate at all, how far it can reach, and how severe the resulting amplification will be.

The mechanism therefore resolves into a structural principle. Systems do not fail in isolation. They fail through the pathways that connect their components. The trigger initiates, the structure propagates, and the system amplifies. Once this progression is recognized, collapse is no longer interpreted as a collection of separate failures or as the oversized consequence of one event alone. It becomes legible as ordered transmission through pre-existing links, intensified by weakness, feedback, and cross-domain spillover.

Failure is not confined to where it begins. It spreads through the connections that already exist within the system.

The Time-to-Failure Compression Mechanism

The Time-to-Failure Compression Mechanism describes a structural change in temporal behavior that begins once instability is active. The central feature is not simply that pressure increases, but that the interval between disruption and breakdown contracts as the system deteriorates. Systems do not fail at a constant rate. The temporal structure of failure changes once instability begins to express itself. Before activation, strain may accumulate slowly and with limited visible consequence. After activation, the same system can move rapidly toward failure because the time available to recognize, process, and respond to worsening conditions begins to shrink.

This makes it necessary to separate time-to-failure from magnitude of stress. Stress matters, but it does not determine outcome by quantity alone. A system can fail faster without a proportional increase in external pressure if its remaining response interval has narrowed. The relevant condition is not only how much strain exists in the structure, but how quickly the system must absorb or resolve that strain relative to its remaining capacity. Time therefore enters as a governing constraint. Failure is shaped by the shrinking interval in which stabilization remains possible.

The difference between slow buildup and rapid collapse follows from this temporal asymmetry. The buildup phase is typically gradual, largely obscured by continuing operation, and structurally quiet in appearance even when underlying strain is increasing. The collapse phase is visible, compressed, and often misread as abrupt because the transition from tolerable instability to overt breakdown occurs after the system's remaining time margin has already narrowed. The pace of visible change in these phases is not symmetrical. Buildup may unfold over a long interval without obvious disorder. Collapse may occur over a much shorter interval because the stored pressure accumulated during the earlier phase becomes active after the system's limits are engaged.

This asymmetry explains why accumulated strain does not express proportionally over time. During the buildup phase, the system can still absorb, defer, or partially mute the consequences of rising pressure. Surface continuity remains intact, even while deeper tolerance is eroding. Once structural limits are engaged, however, that latent strain no longer remains distributed across time in the same way. It converts into rapid change because the system is no longer operating with the same dampening capacity. The long buildup and the short collapse are not separate phenomena. They are different temporal expressions of the same instability process before and after activation.

The crucial distinction is between structural buildup and visible breakdown. Structural buildup refers to the phase in which instability is developing within the system but has not yet forced a visible regime change. Visible breakdown begins when the system can no longer maintain surface continuity at the pace required by its obligations, dependencies, and internal transmission speed. Collapse appears sudden because time compression begins after structural limits are already active. By the time failure becomes unmistakable, much of the temporal compression has already occurred inside the system. The appearance of abruptness comes from the late visibility of a process that had been narrowing response time in advance.

Response time is the interval available for the system to recognize disruption, process its implications, and adapt before conditions worsen further. This interval is not equivalent to elapsed clock time. The system may still be moving through ordinary chronological time, but its usable response time can contract sharply as instability progresses. That contraction occurs because dependencies tighten, sequencing windows narrow, and remaining margins decline. What matters is not how much time exists in an abstract sense, but how much of that time is still structurally usable.

Threshold proximity reduces allowable delay because small postponements become more consequential as the system nears its operating limits. Tight linkages increase the speed with which pressure moves across adjacent components, shortening the interval in which local strain can remain local. Sequential disruption loses its spacing, and the system has less ability to process one problem before the next becomes relevant. These changes do not remove time uniformly. The system still occupies the same hours and days. What it loses is effective response time: the portion of time in which corrective processing remains possible before new pressures enter, options narrow, or deterioration deepens.

This distinction between absolute time and effective response time is essential. Absolute time refers to the objective passage of intervals. Effective response time refers to the actionable portion of those intervals relative to the system's state. A system may nominally have several days before a visible failure point, yet structurally possess far less than that if dependencies are already active, timing conflicts are intensifying, and remaining margin is too thin to absorb delay. In such a condition, the system is operating with less decision space per unit time even though the clock continues normally. Time compression is therefore not a metaphoric claim. It is the contraction of usable temporal capacity relative to ongoing deterioration.

This becomes clearer when considering decision windows. A decision window is the period during which meaningful corrective action remains possible. It is not merely the time in which any response can occur. It is the time in which response still has sufficient leverage over system trajectory. Early-stage instability typically preserves wider decision windows because pressures remain less synchronized, options are broader, and the system still retains multiple pathways for adjustment. Late-stage instability shrinks these windows because timing compresses, dependencies activate together, and the system's available responses lose range and force.

As pressures align within the same interval, sequencing advantages disappear. Several demands may require attention at once. The system cannot process one, restore margin, and then address another with the same effectiveness it would have had earlier. Multiple active constraints crowd into the same operating window, and the effect is not simply a busier interval. It is a reduction in the period during which any response can materially alter outcome. The system may still take action, but the window in which those actions retain stabilizing value is becoming narrower.

The distinction here is between availability of action and effectiveness of action. A response can still be present after the decision window has compressed, but presence alone is not structurally decisive. An action that would have stabilized the system earlier may become insufficient once the window has narrowed, because the surrounding conditions have changed faster than the action can reverse them. This is why late-stage responses often appear ineffective despite resembling earlier responses in form. The issue is not that the system ceased responding. The issue is that the timing context in which response occurs has deteriorated.

Once instability begins to express itself, the rate of deterioration often accelerates. Acceleration, in this context, means that each stage of worsening reduces the system's ability to slow the next stage. Breakdown does not proceed in a straight line. As conditions worsen, the system's remaining ability to absorb, isolate, or defer pressure declines. This causes the next increment of deterioration to arrive more quickly and with greater consequence than the prior one. The system is not merely moving downward. The pace of decline is increasing because the structure's capacity to resist that pace is diminishing.

This distinction separates linear degradation from accelerating breakdown. In linear degradation, each interval produces a roughly comparable reduction in condition. In accelerating breakdown, each interval reduces both stability and the capacity to prevent further rapid decline. The system begins to lose not only strength, but time-adjusted resistance. Once instability is active, the worsening of one component increases the likelihood that adjacent components will deteriorate sooner, and that the system as a whole will have less time to absorb the next sequence of pressures.

The explanation for this acceleration does not depend on new external events arriving at higher magnitude. A system can accelerate toward failure under continuing pressure because its internal capacity to absorb that pressure has changed. The same external burden becomes more destabilizing once remaining tolerance is thinner, transmission is faster, and recovery intervals have shortened. Acceleration is therefore produced by reduced absorbency relative to ongoing strain. The system is not simply declining. It is losing the ability to decline slowly.

Corrective capacity must be understood within this changing temporal structure. Corrective capacity is the system's ability to stabilize itself once disruption has begun. It depends on three conditions: remaining margin, sufficient time to process and act, and enough flexibility to produce responses that still matter. These conditions do not vanish all at once. They deteriorate as instability progresses. The system may retain some ability to intervene even in late stages, but that ability can become insufficient relative to the pace at which conditions are worsening.

As time compresses, remaining margin is consumed faster. Pressures that would once have been spread across wider intervals now arrive in denser sequences. Available options become more constrained because several response routes are either already in use, no longer accessible in time, or too slow relative to the system's rate of deterioration. Interventions may still occur, but they increasingly arrive after the surrounding state has changed. This is the crucial distinction between the presence of intervention and the effectiveness of intervention. Correction is not absent. It becomes temporally mismatched to the speed of instability.

This mismatch is especially important in late-stage conditions. A system can continue attempting to respond while its responses no longer alter trajectory. That is not because the responses are meaningless in abstraction, but because they are arriving inside a structure where thresholds are already engaged, where independent areas of strain are no longer separable, and where transmitted effects are intensifying faster than local corrective measures can offset them. The system is still acting, but the timing advantage required for those actions to restore stability has been lost. Corrective capacity has not disappeared in form. It has become insufficient in relation to the speed of deterioration.

Time must therefore be reframed as a structural variable rather than a neutral background condition. Time is not simply the medium through which system behavior unfolds. It is part of the system's operating architecture because survivability depends on the relationship between response interval and failure progression. Two systems with similar nominal resources can behave differently if one retains wider usable response windows and the other does not. Static capacity alone does not determine resilience. Time-adjusted capacity does.

This distinction between static capacity and time-adjusted capacity changes how system endurance is understood. Static capacity refers to what the system possesses in nominal terms: resources, buffers, throughput, or general strength. Time-adjusted capacity refers to how much of that nominal strength remains deployable within the interval that failure progression allows. A system may possess significant nominal support and still remain fragile if deterioration is moving faster than that support can be translated into stabilizing effect. Conversely, a system with fewer nominal resources can remain more stable if its timing structure preserves wider response windows and slower progression.

Time interacts with previously established structural properties without requiring their full restatement. Proximity to operating limits shortens tolerance for delay. Tight transmission structure increases the speed with which local strain becomes distributed strain. Sequential progression compresses once multiple domains are active, reducing the spacing between events that might otherwise have been processed independently. Together, these conditions shorten the usable time horizon. The relevant point is not that prior mechanisms exist again in full detail, but that their established presence alters the tempo of failure once instability begins. Time compression is the temporal expression of those already-established structural realities.

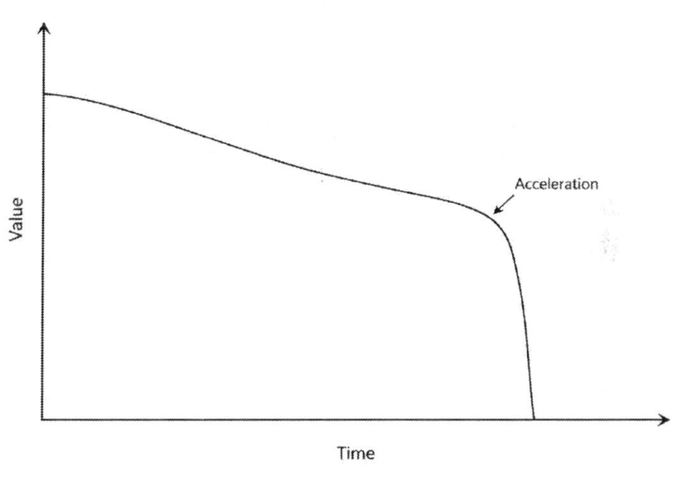

[Figure 8: Time Compression Curve]

The time compression curve clarifies this change in regime. Along the horizontal axis, time proceeds continuously. Along the vertical axis, system stability declines gradually during the buildup phase. That early decline may be shallow enough to remain partly hidden, because the system continues functioning inside a still-operative range. At the compression onset point, the curve inflects. After that point, stability no longer declines at the earlier pace. It turns sharply downward because the structure has entered a compressed regime in which response windows are shorter, corrective capacity is weaker relative to deterioration, and the same continuing pressure now produces faster visible destabilization.

The marked inflection point is therefore not merely a symbolic transition. It identifies the onset of time compression. Before it, the system still possesses enough usable time to distribute stress across longer intervals. After it, the temporal structure changes. The stable zone is defined not by the absence of decline, but by the continued existence of adequate response intervals. The compressed zone begins once those intervals have narrowed enough that deterioration starts outrunning meaningful correction. The curve is steep not because time itself accelerates, but because the system's usable time horizon contracts relative to ongoing failure progression.

This mechanism resolves the difference between slow accumulation and fast collapse without treating them as separate kinds of failure. Accumulation can be slow because stored strain remains partly unexpressed while the system retains enough temporal margin to absorb and defer consequences. Failure progression can be fast because once instability becomes active, the system loses usable time, not merely resources. The visible pace of decline changes because the conditions governing response have changed. The system that once had room to process disruption now confronts disruption in compressed intervals with less leverage over outcome.

The final structural point follows directly. Systems do not fail only because pressure increases. They fail because the time available to respond decreases. Accumulation can be slow. Failure progression is fast. The decisive variable is not only the amount of stress carried, but whether the system can resolve that stress before shrinking response windows, narrowing options, and accelerating deterioration render correction insufficient. Failure is governed not only by the amount of stress a system carries, but by how quickly that stress must be resolved once instability begins.

The Recovery Constraint Mechanism

The Recovery Constraint Mechanism defines recovery as a structurally limited process rather than as an automatic reversal of failure. Once instability has progressed into breakdown, the system that remains is not equivalent to the system that existed before disruption became active. Resources have been consumed, timing has been altered, dependencies have been exposed or tightened, and operating pathways may have been narrowed or damaged. Recovery therefore cannot be understood as the inverse of failure, as though pressure subsides and the system simply retraces its prior path back to stability. The conditions under which recovery begins are already changed by the failure process itself.

This distinction is foundational because it prevents an error that becomes more common in late-stage analysis: the assumption that once acute disruption stops intensifying, restoration becomes the default outcome. But cessation of visible deterioration is not identical to restored capacity. A system can stop worsening rapidly and still remain far from recoverable stability because the configuration from which recovery must proceed has been altered. The relevant question is not whether pressure has begun to subside, but what structural condition remains after failure has imposed depletion, damage, and constraint. Recovery is bounded by what remains, not by what previously existed.

The system after failure is therefore not just a weakened version of its earlier state. It is a different operating condition. Margin may be lower, liquidity thinner, flexibility narrower, and timing tolerance more fragile. Some pathways that previously existed may no longer be available at all, while others may remain available only at much higher cost or with much lower effectiveness. This means recovery capacity cannot be evaluated against the memory of prior stability. It must be evaluated within the altered structure that failure has produced. The system does not recover from a neutral position. It recovers from a damaged one.

Recovery capacity can be defined as the system's ability to restore continuity, rebuild margin, and re-establish stable operation after disruption. This ability depends on three broad conditions: remaining resources, preserved structure, and available time. Remaining resources determine what inputs are still available to support rebuilding. Preserved structure determines whether the system retains enough viable pathways, functional continuity, and organizational integrity to translate inputs into restoration. Available time determines whether those rebuilding processes can occur before further strain, operational demands, or residual instability erode the basis for recovery. None of these conditions can be assumed intact after failure. Failure reduces them simultaneously.

This simultaneity matters because recovery begins from a diminished state, not from a partial pause inside intact operation. Resources that might have supported rebuilding may already have been consumed during stabilization attempts or emergency continuity maintenance. Structural pathways that once carried support efficiently may have been damaged, narrowed, or rendered unreliable by the breakdown process. Time that might have permitted gradual restoration may already have been compressed by the pace at which obligations, operating requirements, or residual strains continue to apply pressure. Recovery capacity must therefore be distinguished from recovery possibility in the abstract. A system may retain theoretical potential to improve while lacking sufficient actual capacity to carry that improvement through to renewed stability.

This is the difference between potential recovery and actual recoverable capacity. Potential recovery refers to the conceptual possibility that the system could improve from its damaged state. Actual recoverable capacity refers to the degree to which the remaining structure, inputs, and time horizon are sufficient to make that improvement materially achievable. The existence of some remaining pathway does not imply enough capacity to use it effectively. A system may still have inflow, still possess assets, still maintain some operational continuity, or still retain some margin for adjustment, yet none of these alone establish that restored stability is structurally reachable. Recovery capacity must be measured against the damaged state itself, not against the fact that some functions remain alive.

This becomes clearer once post-failure recovery is observed across components. Systems do not recover evenly. Income, liquidity, assets, obligations, and operations do not restore at the same rate, through the same process, or with the same degree of friction. Uneven recovery describes this differential restoration across domains. Some components can stabilize relatively quickly because they are less damaged, more directly repairable, or less structurally dependent on other impaired areas. Others remain constrained for much longer because they require the prior restoration of conditions that are themselves still missing. Recovery therefore does not proceed as a synchronized return across the system. It proceeds unevenly, and that unevenness becomes one of the main constraints on total restoration.

A component with faster recovery does not automatically compensate for a slower recovering one if the slower one remains critical to overall system continuity. Liquidity may partially stabilize before income continuity is restored. Operations may resume in limited form while obligations remain binding and inflexible. Certain asset values may recover on paper while access or convertibility remains impaired. These improvements can be real, but they do not by themselves re-establish system-wide stability if the components governing critical continuity remain constrained. The system's condition is therefore determined less by its best-recovering segments than by the slowest recovering critical component.

This establishes the distinction between local recovery and system-level recovery. Local recovery refers to improvement within a specific domain. System-level recovery requires enough restoration across the critical structure that continuity can be maintained without renewed instability. A system may show meaningful localized improvement and still remain structurally unstable because its governing bottlenecks have not yet recovered. Partial restoration can therefore coexist with ongoing fragility. This is why visible improvement in one area often overstates the degree of real recovery if the remaining unresolved components still control whether stable operation is possible.

The structural consequence is that recovery must be evaluated according to dependency order, not just by counting which domains have improved. If a fast-recovering component depends on a slow-recovering critical one, then the system remains constrained by the slower segment regardless of visible gains elsewhere. This is especially important because post-failure analysis can mistake movement for restoration. A domain that begins functioning again may create the impression that stability is returning. But if the components that govern financing, timing, access, or baseline continuity remain impaired, that movement is not yet equivalent to restored operating range. Partial recovery does not equal restored stability when critical constraints remain unresolved.

Time introduces another asymmetry. Breakdown and rebuilding do not proceed according to mirrored temporal rules. Time asymmetry refers to the difference between the speed of collapse and the speed of recovery. Failure can occur rapidly once initiated because instability compresses response time, narrows options, and accelerates propagation across already weakened structure. Recovery does not possess an equivalent acceleration dynamic. Rebuilding margin, restoring capacity, and re-establishing flexibility generally require extended intervals because they depend on sequential restoration rather than on rapid transmission of damage.

This asymmetry means that systems can deteriorate faster than they can rebuild. Structural decline often accelerates once instability begins because each stage of worsening reduces the system's ability to slow the next. Recovery lacks this kind of self-accelerating gain. Improvement typically requires usable resources, viable pathways, preserved continuity, and enough elapsed time for rebuilding to accumulate rather than be immediately consumed. What was lost rapidly often returns only gradually, if at all, because restoration must occur within a still-constrained environment rather than under neutral conditions. The difference between collapse dynamics and recovery dynamics is therefore not only directional. It is temporal and structural.

This distinction matters because post-failure expectation often assumes some rough symmetry between decline and restoration. If breakdown occurred over a short interval, there is often an implicit assumption that equivalent progress in the other direction should also be possible within a similarly compressed period. But collapse and recovery are governed by different mechanics. Collapse exploits existing vulnerability, transmits through connected structure, and can accelerate through narrowing tolerance. Recovery must rebuild what collapse depleted, and it must do so while operating under those depleted conditions. The system therefore does not move back through the same process in reverse. It moves through a slower, more constrained dynamic in which each gain must be preserved before the next can matter.

Resource depletion intensifies this difficulty because recovery is not a neutral process. Recovery consumes resources. It is often described as though it were purely restorative, but structurally it draws from the remaining capacity of the damaged system. Liquidity used to stabilize one part of the structure is no longer available elsewhere. Time devoted to reconstruction cannot simultaneously preserve every prior function.

Operational effort consumed in maintaining continuity under strain is not free input. Recovery is therefore not simply the return of lost strength. It is also the expenditure of what remains.

This produces a distinction between recovery as restoration and recovery as consumption. Restoration refers to the rebuilding of continuity, margin, or functional viability. Consumption refers to the fact that such rebuilding requires inputs that are taken from the already diminished post-failure structure. These inputs may include liquidity, flexibility, retained operational capacity, preserved access, or remaining timing slack. Because the system begins from depletion, the resources used for recovery are drawn from a smaller base than before failure. This means recovery can itself introduce secondary strain if the available inputs are too limited relative to what restoration requires.

The consequence is that the system must rebuild while operating with fewer available inputs than before failure. This creates internal competition. Resources directed toward rebuilding are not available for every other function that still requires support. In heavily constrained post-failure conditions, the act of recovery can therefore intensify local pressure even when it is improving long-run viability. This is not a contradiction. It reflects the fact that the remaining system is still trying to operate while attempting to restore itself. Rebuilding consumes capacity inside the same structure that is already short of it.

This makes resource sufficiency during recovery a relational issue rather than a binary one. The system may still possess resources, but what matters is whether those resources exceed the combined demands of ongoing operation and restorative effort. If they do not, then recovery remains structurally weak even if some rebuilding activity is visible. A system can therefore remain trapped in a condition where every attempt to restore stability consumes inputs faster than restored stability can be re-established. The presence of effort is not enough. The remaining base must be large and durable enough to support both continuity and reconstruction at once.

Path dependency further constrains post-failure recovery. Path dependency refers to the condition in which future options are limited by the sequence of events and responses that occurred during failure. The system does not emerge from breakdown into a field of open possibilities. Its available paths are shaped by what was depleted, what was preserved, what was delayed, and which responses were taken under pressure. Certain routes that might once have existed may now be unavailable, prohibitively costly, or structurally incompatible with the altered state of the system. Recovery thus unfolds along constrained paths, not along all theoretically imaginable ones.

This means the system cannot return to all prior configurations. Some of the conditions that existed before failure depended on margins, timing relationships, and dependency structures that no longer remain intact. Others may technically still be reachable but only through restoration sequences that exceed current capacity. Prior depletion narrows options. Timing shifts alter what can be sequenced effectively. Changed dependencies create new bottlenecks. Structural damage may eliminate entire pathways of restoration that would have been possible earlier. Recovery therefore follows what remains feasible, not what was formerly available.

The distinction is between theoretical recovery and feasible recovery pathways. Theoretical recovery assumes the system could, in principle, reconstitute prior stability if enough improvement occurred. Feasible recovery asks which routes remain structurally open given the actual post-failure state. This distinction is critical because post-failure analysis often overstates recoverability by referencing the full range of pre-failure possibilities. But the system after failure does not possess the same route map. Decisions made under pressure, along with the sequence of loss and stabilization, have already shaped the future landscape of options. What remains possible is conditioned by what has already happened.

Path dependency also means that recovery is not simply constrained by damage, but by the order in which damage and response occurred. Two systems experiencing similar end-state losses may still face different recovery trajectories if they arrived there through different sequences. The ordering of depletion, timing disruption, forced adjustments, and preserved continuity matters because sequence determines which capabilities remain intact and which have been consumed or altered. Recovery is therefore not only limited by amount lost, but by how the failure process reorganized the structure on the way down.

When these elements are taken together, recovery appears not as a self-restoring tendency but as a constrained process. It is bounded by reduced capacity, uneven restoration across critical components, slower temporal dynamics, the resource consumption required to rebuild, and the narrowed pathways that remain feasible after failure. None of these constraints requires re-expansion of earlier mechanisms. Their effects persist into recovery as already-established structural conditions. What matters now is that failure does not terminate cleanly at the point where visible deterioration slows. It carries forward into the rebuilding phase through the altered state it has imposed.

This is why recovery is not guaranteed even if pressure subsides. A decline in active stress does not automatically restore what failure consumed or damaged. The system must operate within the limits created by its own breakdown process. If remaining capacity is too low, if restoration is too uneven, if time asymmetry remains severe, if rebuilding consumes what little flexibility remains, or if the feasible pathways forward are too narrow, then recovery remains structurally constrained regardless of whether acute pressure has eased. The absence of fresh deterioration is not equivalent to regained stability.

The deeper implication is that failure extends into recovery. It does not end when disruption stops accelerating. It continues through constrained rebuilding because the post-failure system carries the residue of the failure process in its altered structure. The system after failure is not simply waiting to recover. It is attempting recovery from inside the losses, depletions, altered dependencies, and compressed pathways that failure itself produced. These conditions are not external to recovery. They define it.

Recovery is therefore not a return to prior conditions. It is a constrained process defined by what the system has lost, what it retains, and what remains structurally possible.

The Concentration Reduction Mechanism

The Concentration Reduction Mechanism describes a structural adjustment in which dependency is redistributed away from narrow points of reliance and spread across a broader set of inputs, channels, and functional supports. The mechanism does not operate by removing dependency altogether. Systems remain dependent by design. Instead, it changes how much each dependency matters. The shift is from a condition where continuity is governed by a small number of heavily loaded nodes to one where reliance is distributed across multiple nodes, each carrying a smaller portion of total system function.

This distinction separates concentration from distribution without treating one as a simple inversion of the other. Concentration describes the accumulation of dependency weight into a limited number of points. Concentration reduction describes the redistribution of that weight without necessarily increasing total resources or altering the system's overall exposure. The adjustment is structural rather than additive. It does not require the system to possess more inputs in absolute terms, although that can occur. It requires that the system's reliance be allocated differently across the inputs it does have. Stability is therefore influenced not only by how much support exists, but by how that support is distributed.

The system becomes less sensitive to disruption when no single point governs a disproportionate share of continuity. Reduced concentration lowers consequence per disruption because each individual dependency carries less weight. A failure at one node still matters, but it matters less than it would in a concentrated configuration. The effect is not the elimination of risk. It is the redistribution of consequence across more points of potential failure. Stability, in this context, is a function of reduced dominance per dependency rather than absence of dependency.

Dependency distribution can be defined as the allocation of system reliance across multiple inputs, channels, or pathways rather than concentrating it in a few. Each dependency contributes to maintaining system continuity. When the number of dependencies increases, or when reliance is more evenly distributed across them, the load borne by each individual dependency decreases. This does not mean each dependency becomes unimportant. It means each becomes less singularly decisive. The system's continuity becomes the result of multiple smaller contributions rather than a few dominant ones.

The distinction between number of dependencies and dependency weight is critical. A system may have several inputs while still being highly concentrated if most of its functional reliance rests on one or two of them. Conversely, a system with fewer total inputs may still achieve meaningful distribution if reliance is more evenly balanced across them. Distribution is therefore not defined by count alone. It is defined by how much continuity is assigned to each node. The structural question is not how many dependencies exist, but how much each dependency governs system outcome.

Within the existing structure, concentration increases consequence per failure because the system allocates a large share of continuity to a small number of points. Distribution reduces exposure to any single disruption by lowering that share. A failure still introduces pressure, but the magnitude of its impact is smaller relative to total system function. The system retains continuity through the remaining dependencies, which continue operating without needing to absorb the entire lost capacity at once.

This produces a proportional effect. As dependency weight is spread, the system's reaction to disruption becomes more proportional to the size of the disturbance rather than being magnified by concentration. When a heavily loaded node fails in a concentrated system, the loss is immediately large because that node governed a significant portion of continuity. When a less heavily loaded node fails in a distributed system, the loss is smaller and can be absorbed or compensated across remaining pathways. Stability improves when dependency weight is spread rather than accumulated, because consequence is reduced at the point of failure.

The same principle applies when examining reliance on single inputs. A dominant input is one that carries a large share of system continuity. When such dominance exists, disruption at that input produces disproportionate impact because the system has assigned it too much structural importance. Reducing reliance on that input does not require eliminating it. It requires lowering its share of total dependency. The system retains the input, but no longer depends on it to the same extent.

This distinction is often misread as a binary condition: either a system relies on a single input or it does not. In practice, reliance exists on a spectrum. A system may technically have multiple inputs but still be dominated by one if the majority of continuity flows through it. Reducing concentration therefore means redistributing reliance so that no input carries an overwhelming portion of system function. The presence of multiple inputs is not sufficient. Their relative importance must be balanced.

When reliance is distributed, disruption at one input produces smaller system impact because continuity is not concentrated there. Remaining inputs continue to support operation, and the system does not experience immediate structural destabilization from a single point failure. This does not eliminate the need for adjustment. It changes the scale of adjustment required. Instead of replacing a dominant share of continuity at once, the system compensates for a smaller portion, which can be absorbed more effectively within its existing tolerance.

The distinction is therefore between the presence of multiple inputs and balanced reliance across them. A system with multiple inputs but concentrated dependency still behaves like a single-input system under stress. A system with balanced reliance behaves differently because each node's failure carries less consequence. Multiple inputs improve stability only when dependency is not concentrated among them. The reduction in consequence per disruption is what alters system sensitivity.

Structural diversification extends this idea beyond input count into the configuration of support pathways. Structural diversification is the distribution of support across distinct functional pathways rather than across superficially different categories. Systems often appear diversified because they include different forms of input or activity, but those forms may still depend on the same underlying conditions. When underlying dependencies are shared, diversification at the surface does not translate into distributed reliance at the structural level.

The distinction between surface diversity and structural independence becomes relevant here. Surface diversity refers to variation in category, form, or appearance. Structural independence refers to the absence of shared dependencies that would cause those varied elements to behave similarly under stress. A system may appear diversified because it includes multiple categories of input, yet remain structurally concentrated if those categories rely on the same timing conditions, access channels, or capacity constraints. In such cases, dependency has not been distributed in a meaningful sense. It has been relabeled.

Structural diversification therefore requires that dependencies be separated at the level of underlying support conditions. If multiple inputs depend on the same constraint, they remain linked despite their apparent differences. Distribution occurs only when dependencies are not only multiple, but also structurally distinct in how they are supported. This does not require complete isolation between components, but it requires that no single underlying condition governs a disproportionate share of system continuity.

This is why diversification improves stability only when dependencies are not shared at the structural level. If multiple inputs fail together because they depend on the same condition, the system behaves as though it were concentrated despite having multiple forms of input. The purpose of distribution is not variety for its own sake. It is the reduction of dependency weight at any single point of structural support. When that reduction is achieved, the system's response to disruption becomes less aligned and less severe.

Reducing concentration has a direct effect on system sensitivity. Sensitivity can be defined as the degree to which system stability changes in response to disruption at a single point. In a highly concentrated system, sensitivity is high because each node carries significant weight. Disruption at one node produces a large change in overall condition. In a distributed system, sensitivity is lower because each node carries less weight. Disruption still produces change, but that change is smaller relative to total system stability.

Lowering sensitivity does not eliminate the system's response to disruption. It redistributes that response across more nodes. Each individual disruption produces a smaller effect, and the system retains more of its continuity. This alters how pressure moves through the structure. Instead of one failure immediately affecting the entire system, disruption remains more localized before it propagates further. The system has more opportunity to absorb, offset, or reallocate strain because no single point failure overwhelms its capacity at once.

The distinction here is between absolute exposure and sensitivity per node. Absolute exposure refers to the total amount of risk or dependency within the system. Sensitivity per node refers to how much any one point contributes to that exposure. Distribution reduces sensitivity per node even if total exposure remains unchanged. This means the system can carry similar levels of overall dependency while being less vulnerable to single-point disruption. The effect is not the removal of risk, but its dilution across more components.

Lower sensitivity produces more proportional absorption of disruption. The system's response becomes aligned with the size of the disturbance rather than being amplified by concentration. A localized failure remains more contained because it does not immediately represent a large share of system continuity. This does not prevent further propagation, but it reduces the initial magnitude of that propagation. Stability improves because the system's reaction becomes more gradual and less dominated by any single failure event.

This structural adjustment introduces trade-offs between efficiency and resilience. Concentration often produces calm-state efficiency because it streamlines pathways, reduces coordination requirements, and concentrates throughput into fewer channels. Distributed structures, by contrast, introduce redundancy, require coordination across more nodes, and may leave some capacity underutilized during normal operation. The system may appear less optimized in calm conditions because it is not maximizing output through the most direct or narrow pathways.

Efficiency favors narrow, streamlined configurations because they minimize complexity and maximize utilization of key inputs. Resilience favors distributed configurations because they reduce dependency weight and preserve continuity under disruption. These priorities operate under different structural criteria. A configuration that appears efficient when conditions are stable may be more sensitive to disruption because it relies heavily on a few critical points. A configuration that appears less efficient may be more stable because it spreads dependency across multiple supports.

This is the distinction between operational efficiency and structural stability. Operational efficiency evaluates performance under calm conditions. Structural stability evaluates behavior under disruption. Reducing concentration shifts the system toward the latter by redistributing dependency. This may increase coordination requirements and reduce apparent simplicity, but it lowers consequence per failure. Efficiency and resilience are therefore not mutually exclusive, but they do not optimize the same structural dimension.

The adjustment toward distribution does not eliminate risk. It redistributes it. The system continues to operate under exposure to disruption, but that exposure is spread across more pathways. When failure occurs, its impact is less dominant at any single point. The system absorbs disruption more proportionally because no individual dependency governs a large share of continuity. This redistribution alters how instability develops rather than removing its possibility.

Within the structure already established, reduced concentration weakens the intensity of failure propagation by lowering the initial magnitude of disruption at any one node. It reduces alignment of failure across dependencies by limiting shared dominance. It increases tolerance to disruption by preserving more continuity after a local failure. These effects operate without requiring full re-expansion of prior mechanisms. They reflect how redistribution changes the system's response characteristics.

The central outcome is that stability is not created by eliminating dependency. It is created by distributing it. Reduced concentration lowers consequence per disruption by ensuring that no single failure point carries enough weight to determine overall system outcome. Continuity becomes the product of multiple contributing nodes rather than the preservation of a few dominant ones. The system remains dependent, but its dependency is structured in a way that reduces sensitivity to any single disruption.

Stability increases not when dependency disappears, but when no single dependency carries enough weight to determine system outcome.

The Absorptive Capacity Mechanism

The Absorptive Capacity Mechanism defines the system's ability to withstand disruption without entering instability as a function of available buffers and how those buffers are structured across layers. Absorptive capacity is not the absence of stress. It is the system's ability to receive, contain, and dissipate stress without allowing that stress to convert into broader structural breakdown. This distinction is essential because systems are continuously exposed to variation. Stability does not arise from eliminating that variation, but from the presence of sufficient structural tolerance to absorb it without transmission.

Buffers form the basis of this tolerance. They are not incidental or optional reserves that exist outside the system's primary function. They are embedded components of the system's architecture that allow continuity to persist under changing conditions. Without buffers, any variation—however small—must be transmitted through the structure because there is no capacity to contain it locally. With buffers, variation can be absorbed, delayed, or dissipated before it affects the wider system. Absorptive capacity therefore emerges from the depth, distribution, and accessibility of buffers across different operational layers.

Buffers can be understood as stored tolerance within the system. They represent the ability to accommodate deviation from expected conditions without immediate structural consequence. This tolerance may exist in the form of readily usable resources, delayed-access capacity, or structural flexibility embedded within the system's design. What unifies these forms is not their category, but their function. Each buffer allows the system to maintain continuity under stress by providing space—either in time, capacity, or optionality—through which disruption can be processed rather than transmitted.

Capacity layers define how these buffers are organized. Immediate buffers are those that can be deployed without delay. They operate at the surface level of the system, where disruption first appears, and they convert immediate strain into manageable variation. Intermediate buffers require some form of conversion or sequencing before they become usable. They extend the system's tolerance beyond the initial layer but are dependent on timing alignment to be effective. Structural buffers exist at a deeper level and include flexibility, timing slack, and optionality embedded in the system's configuration. These do not function as direct inputs, but as adaptive capacity that allows the system to reconfigure itself under pressure.

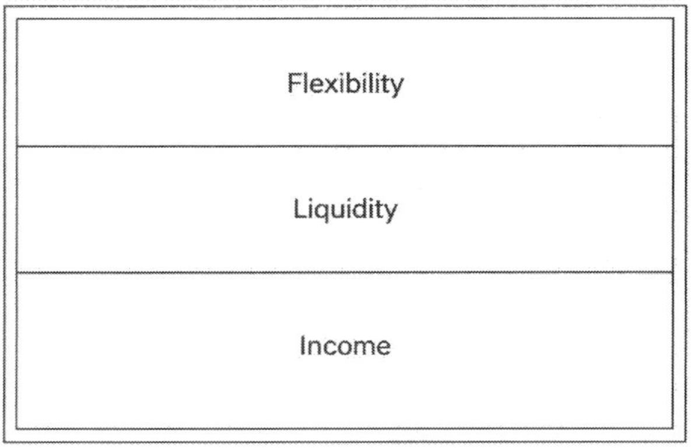

[Figure 9: Absorptive Capacity Layers]

These layers exist simultaneously. Absorptive capacity is not determined by any single layer in isolation, but by how these layers interact. A system may possess substantial total capacity, yet lack absorptive effectiveness if that capacity is concentrated in layers that are inaccessible when needed. Immediate buffers may be shallow while deeper buffers are substantial but slow to deploy. Structural flexibility may exist, but without sufficient immediate support, it may not be actionable within required timeframes. Total capacity therefore does not equal usable capacity. The relevant condition is whether buffers are available, accessible, and coordinated across layers in a way that allows disruption to be absorbed before it propagates.

This introduces a distinction between the presence of resources and the usability of buffers under stress. A system can appear well-resourced in aggregate while lacking sufficient absorptive capacity because those resources cannot be deployed in the required timeframe or are concentrated in forms that do not align with the nature of incoming disruption. Not all stored capacity is accessible when needed. Absorptive capacity depends on whether buffers can be activated at the point where stress enters the system, not simply on whether those buffers exist in abstract form.

The functional consequence is that buffers determine whether disruption is contained or transmitted. When buffers are sufficient and properly structured, disruption remains localized. It is processed within the initial layer where it occurs, and the system continues operating without significant structural change. When buffers are insufficient or inaccessible, disruption moves beyond its point of origin. It enters the system's dependency pathways and begins to affect additional components. Stability is therefore not determined by whether disruption occurs, but by whether it is absorbed before it propagates.

Three primary buffer types define the system's absorptive capacity: liquidity, flexibility, and margin. These are not separate systems, but interdependent forms of structural tolerance that operate together. Liquidity represents the immediate ability to bridge timing gaps. It converts disruption into delay rather than failure by providing the system with usable time to process variation. Without liquidity, timing mismatches translate directly into instability because there is no buffer to absorb the gap between inflow and outflow, demand and capacity, or obligation and fulfillment.

Flexibility represents the system's ability to adjust its structure under pressure. This includes the ability to alter timing, sequence operations differently, reallocate resources, or modify pathways in response to changing conditions. Flexibility does not provide direct capacity in the same way liquidity does. It provides adaptive capacity, allowing the system to reconfigure itself so that existing buffers can be used more effectively. Without flexibility, buffers may exist but remain poorly aligned with the form of disruption, reducing their practical effectiveness.

Margin represents the distance between the system's operating state and its structural limits. It determines how much variation can be absorbed before instability begins. Margin does not absorb disruption directly. It defines how much disruption can be absorbed by other buffers before the system's limits are engaged. A system with thin margin may still possess liquidity and flexibility, but it has less tolerance for cumulative variation. Small disturbances accumulate more quickly into instability because the system is already operating close to its limits.

These three buffer types are interdependent. Loss in one compresses the effectiveness of the others. Reduced liquidity shortens the time available for flexibility to operate. Reduced flexibility limits the system's ability to deploy liquidity efficiently. Reduced margin increases the speed at which both liquidity and flexibility must operate to maintain stability. Absorptive capacity therefore depends not only on the quantity of each buffer, but on their coordination. A system with significant liquidity but low flexibility may struggle to deploy that liquidity effectively. A system with flexibility but minimal margin may not have enough tolerance to use that flexibility before limits are reached.

This introduces a distinction between static capacity and deployable capacity within time constraints. Static capacity refers to the total amount of resources, flexibility, and margin present in the system. Deployable capacity refers to how much of that capacity can be activated within the timeframe required to absorb disruption. Absorptive capacity depends on the latter. A system may appear robust in static terms while remaining fragile in dynamic conditions if its buffers cannot be deployed in time or in coordination.

The difference between absorptive and transmissive systems emerges from this structure. Absorptive systems dampen disruption locally. Incoming stress is converted into delay, adjustment, or partial loss that remains contained within the initial layer. The system continues operating because the disruption does not propagate into deeper structural pathways. Transmissive systems, by contrast, lack sufficient buffering. Disruption enters the system and moves through dependencies, turning local variation into broader structural pressure. Continuity degrades because the system cannot contain the initial disturbance.

The same disruption can produce different outcomes depending on buffer presence and structure. In an absorptive system, the disruption is processed and dissipated. In a transmissive system, the disruption becomes the starting point for propagation. The mechanism that determines this difference is not the magnitude of the disruption itself, but the system's ability to convert that disruption into manageable variation. Buffers perform this conversion. Without them, the system cannot translate disruption into delay or adjustment, and transmission becomes the default outcome.

This distinction emphasizes that stability is determined by what happens after disruption enters the system. Disruption is not the decisive event. The decisive process is how the system receives it. Buffers convert shock into forms that can be managed. Absence of buffers converts shock into propagation. The system's behavior under stress is therefore defined by its absorptive capacity rather than by the presence or absence of disruption.

Layered defense structures extend this principle by organizing buffers across multiple levels of intensity. The outer layer absorbs minor variation. It operates continuously, smoothing small fluctuations before they accumulate. The middle layer handles moderate disruption that exceeds the capacity of the outer layer. It engages when variation becomes too large to be absorbed at the surface. The core layer protects system continuity under severe stress. It represents the final buffer before structural instability occurs.

These layers are sequential rather than redundant. Each operates at a different scale and with different characteristics of speed, cost, and capacity. The outer layer is fast and low-cost but limited in depth. The middle layer is slower and more resource-intensive but provides greater capacity. The core layer is the most resource-intensive and often the slowest to deploy, but it carries the greatest importance because it determines whether the system maintains continuity under extreme conditions.

Failure occurs when disruption penetrates multiple layers without being absorbed. If the outer layer is insufficient, disruption moves to the middle layer. If the middle layer is insufficient, it reaches the core. Once the core layer is overwhelmed, the system enters instability because no further buffering remains. The presence of multiple layers allows the system to degrade gradually, absorbing disruption at successive levels. Without layered buffering, disruption moves directly to deeper structural pathways, producing more abrupt instability.

This creates a distinction between single-layer buffering and multi-layer buffering. Systems with a single layer of buffering may handle minor variation effectively but become vulnerable once that layer is exceeded. Systems with layered buffers have multiple opportunities to absorb disruption, each with different characteristics. As established earlier, transmission pathways determine how quickly disruption reaches deeper layers, but the presence of layers determines whether it is absorbed before reaching them. Systems with layered buffers degrade progressively. Systems without them transition more abruptly from stability to instability.

Capacity exhaustion describes the progressive depletion of buffers over time. Exhaustion occurs when buffers are consumed faster than they can be replenished. This is not a binary condition. It develops in stages. In the early stage, buffers absorb disruption without visible consequence. The system appears stable because variation is being contained within existing capacity. In the middle stage, buffers begin to thin. The system becomes more sensitive because less capacity remains to absorb additional variation. In the late stage, buffers are exhausted. Disruption can no longer be contained and begins to propagate through the structure.

Exhaustion reduces both capacity and response time. As buffer depth declines, the system has less tolerance for delay and less ability to absorb additional stress. Previously contained disruptions begin to propagate once buffer depth falls below functional thresholds. This transition is often not visible until it occurs because the early and middle stages of exhaustion maintain surface stability. The system appears unchanged while its absorptive capacity is declining.

This introduces a distinction between buffer presence and remaining buffer depth. The system may still possess buffers, but their depth may be insufficient to absorb incoming disruption. Exhaustion is therefore not the absence of buffers, but the reduction of their effectiveness. It is often invisible until transmission begins because the system can continue operating while buffers are being consumed. The visible change occurs only when remaining capacity is no longer sufficient to contain variation.

Accessibility and timing determine whether buffers can function when needed. Buffers that exist but cannot be deployed within required timeframes do not contribute to absorptive capacity in practice. Accessible buffers are those that can be activated within the interval between disruption and structural consequence. Inaccessible buffers may require conversion, sequencing, or conditions that exceed the available time window. Timing mismatch occurs when the system requires buffer deployment before those buffers can be made usable.

This introduces a distinction between total capacity and usable capacity within time constraints. A system may possess substantial total capacity but remain vulnerable if that capacity is not accessible at the moment of disruption. Resources that require conversion may not be usable if conversion exceeds the available response interval. Capacity that exists in theory may not exist in practice if it cannot be deployed in time. Absorptive capacity is therefore time-dependent. It depends on whether buffers are not only present, but also available within the timeframe required to absorb disruption.

Buffer depth defines the total usable capacity available before the system enters instability. Greater depth allows the system to absorb more disturbances, whether sequentially or concurrently. Lower depth reduces the number of disturbances required to trigger instability. Depth is not solely a measure of volume. It includes layering and accessibility. A system with large nominal resources but limited accessibility or poor layering may have less effective depth than a system with smaller but more deployable buffers.

This distinction separates superficial capacity from structurally deployable depth. Superficial capacity refers to total resources without regard to their usability. Structurally deployable depth refers to the portion of capacity that can be activated across layers and within required timeframes. Survivability is proportional to effective buffer depth, not nominal resource size. As established earlier, once operating limits are approached, remaining buffer depth becomes the governing constraint on system behavior.

False signals of capacity arise when systems are evaluated based on nominal resources rather than functional buffering under stress. A system may appear buffered because it possesses visible resources, yet lack sufficient absorptive capacity due to concentration, inaccessibility, timing mismatch, or shared dependency. Visible stability does not imply adequate buffering because it reflects calm-state performance rather than stress-state behavior.

This introduces a distinction between perceived capacity and structural absorptive capacity. Perceived capacity is based on observation of resources under normal conditions. Structural absorptive capacity is based on how those resources function under disruption. Buffers must be evaluated by their ability to absorb stress when it occurs, not by their presence when it does not. Systems may overestimate their stability if they rely on measures that do not account for accessibility, timing, or distribution of buffers.

The mechanism resolves by establishing that systems do not survive because disruption is avoided. They survive because disruption is absorbed without triggering propagation. Absorptive capacity determines whether disruption remains local or becomes systemic. Buffer depth, accessibility, and layering define the limits of survivability. Survival is not determined by the absence of stress, but by the system's capacity to absorb it without losing continuity.

The Downside Limitation Mechanism

The Downside Limitation Mechanism defines stability as the structural restriction of how large failure can become. It does not assume that disruption can be eliminated, nor does it depend on reducing the frequency of adverse events to zero. Instead, it defines control in terms of bounded consequence. Systems remain viable not because failure is absent, but because the effects of failure are constrained within limits that preserve continuity and recoverability. The mechanism shifts the focus from preventing every disruption to ensuring that no single disruption can exceed the system's capacity to absorb, contain, and rebuild.

This reframing establishes that exposure, not occurrence, governs outcome. Loss exposure refers to the maximum potential consequence attached to any point in the system. It is not defined by the likelihood of an event, but by how much continuity depends on the node, pathway, or structure where disruption occurs. Exposure is therefore structural. It exists regardless of whether disruption is currently active. A system may appear stable under calm conditions while still carrying high exposure if significant portions of its continuity are concentrated in a small number of points.

Capping loss exposure operates by reducing the maximum consequence associated with any single failure. The event itself may still occur, but its impact is limited. This limitation is achieved by reducing the amount of system continuity attached to any one dependency, pathway, or operational element. When exposure is capped, the system ensures that the failure of any single component does not translate into a loss large enough to threaten overall viability. The emphasis is not on eliminating failure events, but on bounding their potential impact.

This introduces a distinction between frequency of disruption and magnitude of consequence. A system may experience frequent minor disruptions while remaining stable if each disruption is small relative to its capacity. Conversely, a system may experience infrequent disruption yet still be unstable if any single event can produce a catastrophic outcome. Stability is therefore not determined by how often disruption occurs, but by how large its consequences can become. Systems fail not only because disruption occurs, but because the magnitude of consequence exceeds survivable bounds.

The structural implication is that limitation improves stability by reducing the maximum loss per event. When no single event can produce catastrophic outcome, the system retains continuity even under repeated disruption. This does not eliminate stress, but it prevents stress from accumulating into irreversible damage. Stability emerges when consequence is constrained such that each disruption remains within the system's absorptive and recovery capacity.

Containment extends this principle by restricting how failure spreads beyond its point of origin. Structural containment refers to the system's ability to prevent local disruption from propagating across domains. Failure is not prevented, but it is confined. The system establishes boundaries that limit transmission, ensuring that disruption remains localized rather than becoming system-wide pressure. These boundaries are not reactive measures introduced after failure begins. They are embedded in the system's structure before disruption occurs.

The distinction between local failure and system-wide failure follows directly. A local failure affects a specific node or pathway. A system-wide failure occurs when that disruption spreads through dependencies, affecting multiple components and degrading overall continuity. Containment ensures that failure remains at the local level. It prevents the transformation of a single-point disruption into a multi-domain breakdown. The system continues operating because the disruption does not expand beyond its initial scope.

Containment operates by restricting propagation pathways. As established, failure spreads through existing connections. Limitation constrains those connections so that they cannot transmit unlimited consequence. This does not eliminate connectivity, but it reduces its capacity to carry disruption beyond defined boundaries. Containment transforms structures that would otherwise transmit failure into structures that compartmentalize it. The system becomes segmented in its response to disruption, allowing affected areas to absorb impact without immediately affecting others.

The key effect is that containment changes the scale at which failure operates. Instead of a single disruption escalating into a cascading sequence, it remains confined to a limited portion of the system. Stability increases when failure remains localized because the system retains functional continuity outside the affected area. The system can continue operating while addressing the local disruption, rather than being forced into simultaneous system-wide adjustment.

Limiting the magnitude of negative outcomes extends beyond containment to the scaling of consequence. Magnitude refers to the total system impact resulting from a failure event. It is not solely determined by the size of the initiating disruption. It is shaped by how that disruption is amplified or dampened by the system's structure. Downside limitation reduces amplification potential, ensuring that small disruptions do not expand into disproportionately large outcomes.

This introduces a distinction between event severity and structural consequence. Event severity describes the size of the initial disturbance. Structural consequence describes the total impact after the system has processed that disturbance. A small event can produce large consequence if the system amplifies it. A large event can produce limited consequence if the system constrains its impact. Limitation operates on consequence scaling. It restricts how much amplification can occur, regardless of the initial event size.

The effect is that systems become more stable when consequence scaling is constrained. Disruption remains closer in magnitude to its origin rather than expanding through amplification. This reduces the likelihood that cumulative effects will exceed system capacity. The system absorbs disruption more proportionally, maintaining continuity even when multiple disturbances occur. Stability is therefore influenced not by eliminating events, but by limiting their ability to grow beyond manageable scale.

Preventing irreversible damage represents the most critical function of downside limitation. Irreversibility occurs when failure reaches a state where recovery is no longer structurally feasible. At this point, the system cannot return to stable operation because essential pathways, resources, or capacities have been permanently compromised. Not all failures lead to this state. Some failures are recoverable, allowing the system to rebuild. Others cross into terminal conditions where recovery is no longer possible.

Limitation operates by preserving recoverability. It ensures that failure does not extend beyond the system's capacity to restore continuity. This is achieved by preventing disruption from crossing into regimes where structural damage eliminates recovery pathways. As established, system behavior changes once certain limits are exceeded. Limitation restricts failure from reaching those conditions. It keeps disruption within ranges where rebuilding remains possible.

This introduces a distinction between recoverable loss and terminal loss. Recoverable loss reduces system capacity but leaves sufficient structure intact for recovery. Terminal loss removes critical components or pathways such that recovery cannot proceed. The most important failures to prevent are not those that cause temporary disruption, but those that eliminate the possibility of restoration. Limitation focuses on preserving the system's ability to recover rather than preventing all forms of failure.

This focus on recoverability shifts the definition of stability. Stability is not defined by the absence of loss, but by the preservation of pathways through which loss can be repaired. A system that experiences frequent recoverable losses may remain viable indefinitely. A system that experiences a single terminal loss ceases to function. Limitation ensures that failure remains within recoverable bounds, preserving the system's long-term viability.

Designing for bounded risk formalizes this principle. Bounded risk describes a condition in which the maximum possible loss is constrained within predefined limits. These limits are structural. They define the worst-case outcome that any single disruption can produce. The system is configured so that no dependency, pathway, or node can generate consequence beyond those limits. Boundaries are not predictions about what will occur. They are constraints on what can occur.

This introduces a distinction between open-ended risk and bounded risk. Open-ended risk allows for outcomes that exceed system capacity. Bounded risk restricts outcomes to levels the system can absorb and recover from. Systems with open-ended risk may operate efficiently under normal conditions but remain vulnerable to catastrophic failure. Systems with bounded risk may operate with constraints but maintain continuity under a wider range of conditions.

The structural effect is that systems with bounded risk can withstand repeated disruption without catastrophic failure. Each event is limited in consequence, allowing the system to continue operating and rebuilding. Stability emerges from the accumulation of bounded events rather than from the avoidance of disruption. Control is achieved not by predicting which events will occur, but by ensuring that any event remains within survivable limits.

This introduces a trade-off between opportunity and limitation. Greater limitation constrains exposure, but it may also restrict throughput, efficiency, and peak performance. Systems that concentrate dependency often achieve higher output under stable conditions because they streamline pathways and maximize utilization of key inputs. Limitation reduces this concentration, distributing dependency across more points and thereby reducing exposure per node. This redistribution may introduce redundancy, reduce apparent efficiency, and limit maximum output.

The distinction is between maximization and survivability. Maximization seeks to increase output by concentrating resources and dependencies. Survivability seeks to preserve continuity by limiting exposure. These objectives operate under different structural priorities. A system optimized for maximum output may increase its vulnerability to disruption because it concentrates consequence. A system structured for limitation reduces vulnerability but may operate below its theoretical maximum capacity.

This trade-off does not imply that limitation eliminates opportunity. It indicates that expansion of exposure increases consequence. Systems that increase dependency per node amplify both potential gain and potential loss. Limitation constrains this amplification by reducing dependency concentration. Stability requires accepting constraints on how much exposure can be attached to any single element. The system sacrifices some degree of efficiency in order to preserve continuity under stress.

The distinction between predictive control and structural control becomes relevant here. Predictive control assumes that failure can be avoided through accurate anticipation of events. Structural control assumes that failure cannot be eliminated, and instead focuses on limiting its consequence. Predictive approaches depend on correct identification of future conditions. Structural limitation remains effective regardless of event type because it constrains outcome rather than attempting to predict occurrence.

False control arises when systems assume that prediction or optimization can prevent failure entirely. This assumption overlooks the presence of uncertainty and variability. Systems cannot eliminate uncertainty. They can only limit its effects. Structural limitation provides a form of control that does not depend on forecasting accuracy. It ensures that even unexpected events remain within survivable bounds. This is why limitation remains effective across a wide range of conditions, while predictive strategies may fail when conditions deviate from expectation.

The distinction is between attempting to prevent disruption and ensuring that disruption remains manageable. Predictive control focuses on avoidance. Structural control focuses on containment. True control is achieved by limiting what failure can do, not by assuming failure can be prevented. This distinction becomes more important as systems operate under increasing complexity and uncertainty, where prediction becomes less reliable.

Limitation must be distributed across the system rather than concentrated at a single boundary. A system that limits exposure at one point but leaves other areas unbounded remains vulnerable. Disruption can bypass the limited node and enter through another pathway. Effective limitation requires that exposure be constrained across multiple dependencies, channels, and structural elements. This distribution prevents any single point from carrying enough weight to produce catastrophic outcome.

The distinction is between centralized limitation and distributed limitation. Centralized limitation focuses on restricting risk at specific points. Distributed limitation ensures that all critical nodes and pathways are constrained. The latter reduces the likelihood that unbounded exposure exists anywhere in the system. Stability depends on consistent limitation across structure, not on isolated constraints.

Distributed limitation also reduces concentration of exposure. When limitation is applied across multiple points, dependency is naturally spread, reducing the consequence attached to any single node. This reinforces the relationship between limitation and distribution. Limitation does not operate independently of structure. It reshapes structure by constraining how much reliance can accumulate at any point.

The mechanism resolves by establishing that systems achieve stability not by avoiding all disruption, but by ensuring that disruption cannot escalate beyond survivable limits. Disruption is inevitable. Exposure is structural. Limitation defines whether that exposure can produce catastrophic consequence. Systems remain viable when each failure event is constrained within bounds that preserve continuity and recoverability.

Control is not the ability to prevent failure, but the ability to ensure that failure remains within bounds the system can survive.

The Redundancy & Buffer Layering Mechanism

The Redundancy & Buffer Layering Mechanism defines stability as a function of multiple, overlapping protective structures that preserve continuity when individual components fail. Redundancy introduces alternate pathways through which function can continue. Buffer layering introduces staged absorption through which disruption can be weakened before it reaches system-critical depth. Together, they prevent failure from becoming singular, dominant, and uncontained. The mechanism does not eliminate disruption. It changes what disruption encounters once it enters the structure. Instead of finding one decisive boundary whose breach determines outcome, disruption meets a sequence of defensive conditions that can absorb, redirect, or slow its effects before continuity is lost.

Layered protection begins with the recognition that not all disruption is equal in intensity, speed, or persistence. Systems that preserve stability under varied conditions do not rely on one uniform line of defense. They are structured so that different layers handle different levels of pressure. Outer layers absorb frequent, low-intensity variation. These layers operate quickly and continuously, smoothing disturbances that are too small to justify deeper mobilization. Middle layers engage when disruption exceeds the capacity of the first layer. They are slower, deeper, and more resource-intensive, but they can manage more substantial shocks. Inner layers protect core continuity under severe stress. They are not designed for frequent use. They exist to preserve system survival when outer defenses have already been penetrated.

The distinction between single-line defense and multi-layer defense is decisive. A single-line system depends on one protective boundary to hold. If that boundary fails, disruption reaches the system core without meaningful attenuation. A layered system requires disruption to penetrate multiple stages before it can become systemic. Each layer creates another point at which disturbance can be weakened, delayed, or redirected. The effect is not simply more protection in quantity. It is more protection in sequence. A failure that would have been decisive in a single-line structure becomes only the beginning of a longer process in a layered one.

Each protective layer operates with different characteristics of speed, capacity, and cost. Outer layers tend to be fast and low-cost, because they must respond frequently and cannot consume excessive structural effort each time variation appears. Middle layers tend to have greater capacity and greater activation cost, because they are designed for less frequent but more consequential disturbances. Inner layers carry the highest significance because they preserve continuity when all prior defenses have been partly or fully consumed. Their use is often costly in structural terms, but their purpose is not efficiency. It is survival. This differentiation matters because layered protection is not repetition of the same safeguard. It is stratification of tolerance according to severity and depth of threat.

The structural consequence is that stability increases when no single breach determines system outcome. A disruption may pass through one layer without becoming fatal because further layers remain available. The system does not require perfect defense at the perimeter. It requires enough cumulative depth that the failure of one layer does not immediately imply whole-system breakdown. This is the central advantage of layering. It transforms stability from a binary condition into a graduated one, where protective capacity exists across stages rather than at one decisive point.

Redundancy complements this by expanding the number of pathways through which continuity can be maintained. Redundancy is the presence of alternate routes, substitute functions, or duplicate capacity that allows the system to continue operating when a primary component fails. It is often perceived as excess, underutilization, or inefficiency because calm conditions reveal its idle aspect more readily than its protective role. A redundant component may appear unnecessary while the primary path remains intact. Structurally, however, redundancy is not waste. It is continuity insurance embedded in the architecture.

This distinction separates maximum efficiency from survivability. Systems optimized for maximum efficiency compress function into narrow, highly utilized pathways. Under stable conditions, this compression appears advantageous because it reduces duplication and concentrates output. But the same compression makes failure more consequential because too much continuity depends on too little structure. Redundancy expands the structure. It creates additional routes through which function can continue if a primary route weakens. The system may appear less streamlined, but it is less exposed to singular disruption.

Redundant elements allow substitution and load redistribution. If one node fails, another can absorb part or all of its function. If one channel becomes impaired, continuity can be preserved through an alternate route. This does not require the redundant element to mirror the primary one exactly. What matters is functional continuity, not perfect symmetry. A substitute pathway may differ in cost, speed, or capacity, yet still prevent collapse by keeping the system operational while the failed route is bypassed or restored. Systems optimized only for efficiency often appear strong in calm conditions because their narrow structure performs well under uninterrupted support. Structurally, however, they are fragile because they lack alternate routes once interruption appears.

This leads to the distinction between single systems and parallel systems. A single system relies on one pathway to handle full functional load. Failure in that pathway creates immediate interruption because no alternate structure exists to carry the function. A parallel system distributes or replicates load across multiple pathways. Failure in one path reduces performance, but does not necessarily eliminate continuity. The outcome changes from interruption to degradation. This is not a minor difference in degree. It is a difference in failure form.

Single systems produce binary failure behavior. The pathway works or it does not. Once it fails, continuity is broken because the full load had no alternate route. Parallel systems produce graded degradation. Capacity may decline, throughput may narrow, and efficiency may fall, but the system continues to operate because remaining pathways still carry part of the load. Parallel does not require equal distribution across all paths. It requires sufficient substitution that the loss of one path does not remove total functionality. The consequence of failure is therefore reduced from discontinuity to partial impairment.

The structural importance of this distinction lies in how it changes survivability. A system that can degrade without disappearing possesses more recovery space than one that moves directly from full operation to interruption. Parallel systems convert collapse into performance reduction. That conversion is stabilizing because it preserves continuity under strain. The system is impaired, but not lost. Survivability improves when failure reduces capacity rather than eliminating it, because continuation allows remaining layers and pathways to function instead of being nullified by a single decisive break.

Layered resilience does not depend only on perfectly separate safeguards. Overlapping safeguards also contribute to stability. Overlap refers to protective elements that are not fully independent, but not fully dependent either. They may share partial dependencies, activate under different conditions, or operate at different levels of the system. Their value lies in the fact that their failure modes are not fully aligned. If one safeguard is weakened, others can still retain partial function. This reduces the likelihood that protective failure becomes total and simultaneous.

The distinction here is between perfect independence and functional overlap. Perfect independence is structurally powerful but often difficult to achieve fully. Functional overlap accepts that safeguards may share some conditions while still remaining differentiated enough to prevent complete synchronization of failure. Systems do not require absolute separation in order to achieve resilience. They require sufficient non-alignment that all protective elements do not fail at the same time for the same reason. Overlap fills coverage gaps and preserves partial continuity even when some dependencies are shared.

This matters because protection often fails not when one safeguard is absent, but when several safeguards collapse together. Overlap reduces that risk by ensuring that failure conditions differ enough across the protective structure to prevent full alignment. One safeguard may weaken under one set of conditions while another remains active because its activation logic, load profile, or operating layer differs. Stability improves when safeguards do not fail simultaneously. The system gains resilience not from perfect purity of separation, but from partial differentiation strong enough to break synchronized collapse.

Layering also alters how failure propagates by slowing and weakening its movement through the system. When disruption enters the outer layer, partial absorption occurs there first. Residual pressure that exceeds the outer layer's capacity then moves inward, but it does so in reduced form. The next layer receives not the full original disturbance, but a diminished and often delayed version of it. Additional layers then absorb further portions of the remaining pressure. This sequential attenuation changes both the speed and magnitude of failure progression.

The distinction is between direct transmission and staged attenuation. Direct transmission occurs when disruption reaches system-critical pathways without meaningful reduction along the way. Staged attenuation occurs when each protective layer strips away some portion of the disruption before it moves onward. Each layer reduces magnitude, slows transmission, and narrows propagation potential. The cumulative result is that disruption weakens as it travels rather than retaining full force across each connection.

This is why systems with layers fail gradually while systems without layers fail abruptly. In a layered structure, pressure is progressively degraded as it moves inward. The system has multiple chances to contain or slow the disturbance before continuity is threatened. In an unlayered structure, pressure reaches critical zones too quickly and too completely, making the transition from stability to breakdown much sharper. Layering converts sharp failure into progressive degradation by interrupting the direct path between local disruption and system-wide consequence.

Redundancy adds another form of protection by enabling structural substitution. Its value is not merely in the presence of backup components, but in the ability of those components to assume function when needed. Idle redundancy has limited stabilizing effect if it cannot become operational within the interval required by the disruption. Effective redundancy requires accessibility, compatibility, and timing alignment. The substitute element must be available, structurally capable of carrying the relevant load, and activatable within the window before continuity is lost.

This creates the distinction between idle redundancy and active substitution capacity. Idle redundancy exists but may remain inert under pressure because it cannot be deployed quickly enough, cannot handle the required function, or depends on conditions that are unavailable when failure occurs. Active substitution capacity preserves continuity because the redundant element can actually assume load within the relevant interval. Redundancy is only valuable when it functions as replacement rather than as passive duplication. Its stabilizing role depends on whether it can move from reserve to operation before the system crosses into discontinuity.

Layering and redundancy also interact through load transfer. Protective layers are not isolated compartments. If an outer layer fails or is exhausted, inner layers inherit greater load. If one pathway is impaired, redundant pathways absorb more function. The distinction here is between independent layers and interdependent layers. In practice, protective levels and substitute routes influence one another continuously. The effectiveness of layering depends on whether transferred load remains within the capacity of deeper layers and parallel paths. If outer-layer failure immediately overwhelms inner defenses, layering exists in form but not in function.

This means stability depends on balanced capacity across layers rather than on the mere presence of multiple layers. A system may possess outer, middle, and inner defenses, yet still remain fragile if those defenses are misaligned in depth or load-transfer capacity. Similarly, redundant pathways may exist, yet fail to preserve continuity if the surviving paths cannot absorb the transferred burden. Effective layering requires that load transfer be manageable. Each subsequent layer must be strong enough relative to the burden passed inward, and each alternate path must be capable of carrying enough of the displaced function to prevent collapse.

The same principle applies to dependency distribution across levels. Layering is effective when it spreads burden through stages rather than allowing full load concentration at one depth. If too much load is attached to a single protective layer, the failure of that layer becomes decisive. If load is distributed more proportionally across layers and substitute routes, the system retains more graded behavior under stress. Stability therefore depends not simply on the number of layers, but on the balance of capacity among them.

Failure mode diversity further strengthens this structure. Different layers and redundant elements do not contribute equally if they all fail under identical conditions. Homogeneous protection can create the appearance of depth while retaining synchronized vulnerability. If multiple layers share the same failure trigger, then disruption can penetrate them together rather than sequentially. Stability increases when protection is diversified such that layers, paths, and safeguards fail under different conditions and at different thresholds.

The distinction is between homogeneous protection and diversified protection. Homogeneous protection replicates the same form of defense without materially changing its exposure profile. Diversified protection introduces variation in operating conditions, activation requirements, and failure triggers. The system does not need every layer to be radically different in every respect. It needs enough variation that one form of disruption does not disable all protective elements at once. This de-synchronization is crucial because it preserves staged defense rather than allowing total collapse of protection in a single movement.

Failure mode diversity also clarifies why redundancy cannot be identical replication alone. If the alternate path fails under exactly the same conditions as the primary path, it does not meaningfully reduce vulnerability. Its presence increases count, but not resilience. Effective redundancy includes variation in how and when it fails. This may arise from different timing profiles, different support conditions, or different activation requirements. Stability increases when failures are de-synchronized across layers because the system retains some functioning protection even when one mode of defense is compromised.

The mechanism therefore introduces a trade-off between simplicity and resilience. Simplicity favors fewer paths, lower coordination requirements, and cleaner structural visibility. Layered, redundant systems increase complexity because they introduce more components, more interactions, and more conditions under which substitution or staged absorption must be coordinated. Under calm conditions, simplicity often appears preferable because it reduces administrative friction and preserves clarity of operation. Under stress, however, simplicity can become fragility because it leaves the system with too little defensive depth.

The distinction is between clarity in calm conditions and survivability under disruption. Simplicity improves the former by reducing the number of moving parts. Layering and redundancy improve the latter by ensuring that disruption encounters multiple opportunities to be absorbed, redirected, or slowed. Systems optimized for simplicity often lack these opportunities. Their structure appears elegant while uninterrupted conditions persist, but their defensive depth is shallow once failure begins. They rely too heavily on primary pathways and single-layer protection, making them more exposed to singular and dominant breakdown.

Resilient structures therefore accept greater coordination requirements in exchange for reduced systemic fragility. This is not because complexity is inherently stabilizing, but because protective depth and substitution capacity require more than one path, more than one layer, and more than one mode of functioning under strain. The relevant issue is not complexity for its own sake. It is whether complexity is serving layered defense and alternative continuity rather than merely adding noise. When it does, the structure gains survivability even at the cost of calm-state simplicity.

The mechanism resolves into a clear structural principle. Systems do not avoid disruption. They prevent disruption from becoming singular and dominant. Redundancy provides alternative pathways through which continuity can persist when primary elements fail. Layering provides staged absorption through which disruption is progressively weakened before it reaches the system core. Overlap prevents synchronized failure by ensuring that safeguards do not share complete alignment of failure modes. The result is that failure becomes distributed, slowed, and reduced in consequence.

A stable system, under this mechanism, is not one in which nothing fails. It is one in which failure encounters enough layers and alternatives that collapse is prevented. Singular outcomes are replaced by graded degradation. Immediate interruption is replaced by partial impairment. Direct transmission is replaced by attenuation. System-critical continuity survives because disruption is never allowed to reach it in full force through a single breach.

Systems do not remain stable because nothing fails, but because failure encounters enough layers and alternatives to prevent collapse.

The Liquidity Interaction Mechanism

The Liquidity Interaction Mechanism defines liquidity not as a static stock of funds, but as financial time: the interval a system can continue operating before failure occurs under current conditions. Liquidity matters because it converts structural condition into duration. It determines how long obligations can be met, how long operations can continue, how long dependencies can remain supported, and how long instability can be managed before continuity breaks. This reframing is necessary because nominal resource size alone does not describe survivability. A system can hold meaningful resources and still possess little effective runway if those resources are consumed rapidly under active strain. Liquidity is therefore not only a buffer. It is the primary variable through which structural exposure becomes time-bound.

This establishes the distinction between nominal resources and time-adjusted survival capacity. Nominal resources describe the quantity of funds or usable inputs present in the system. Time-adjusted survival capacity describes how long those inputs can sustain continuity under current burn conditions. The two are not equivalent. A larger nominal resource base does not guarantee longer survival if operating pressure is high enough to consume that base quickly. A smaller nominal base may sustain continuity for longer if pressure remains modest and depletion is controlled. Liquidity must therefore be measured not just by amount, but by duration. The key question is not how much the system holds in abstract terms, but how long that holding preserves function under present conditions.

Liquidity translates capacity into time. This is its defining role. Resources on their own are static. Liquidity expresses how those resources interact with obligations, inflows, operating demands, and active instability across an interval. More liquidity means longer runway because the system can continue funding continuity for a longer period before depletion. Less liquidity means shorter runway because the interval between current operation and failure is narrower. The relevance of liquidity is therefore temporal before it is monetary. It tells the system how much time remains before structural limits become operational consequences.

This is why survival is governed by remaining time, not total resources alone. Total resources matter only insofar as they can sustain continuity over the period required for stabilization, adjustment, or recovery. If they cannot extend that interval sufficiently, then their nominal size overstates their practical value. A system does not fail when it reaches theoretical insufficiency in the abstract. It fails when remaining liquidity no longer buys enough time for the system to continue functioning under its current pressure level. Liquidity is therefore the mechanism through which survivability becomes measurable in time units rather than only in resource units.

Risk interacts with this process by determining how quickly liquidity is consumed. Within the already established structure, risk can be understood as active pressure on the system: financial pressure, operational strain, structural instability, and the ongoing consequences of misalignment across dependencies. The important point here is that risk does not only threaten future failure in a conceptual sense. It changes the speed at which the system burns through its remaining time. High risk is not only dangerous because it increases the chance of bad outcomes. It is dangerous because it accelerates depletion.

This creates the distinction between static runway and dynamic runway. Static runway assumes that the system's survival interval can be measured by dividing current liquidity by a stable burn rate, as though both the structure and the pressure acting on it remain constant. Dynamic runway recognizes that the burn rate changes as conditions change. Runway is not fixed. It is a moving interval that expands or contracts according to the interaction between available liquidity and active risk intensity. Two systems with identical liquidity can therefore have radically different survival times if one is under mild strain and the other is under escalating pressure.

Higher risk increases depletion rate. Lower risk slows it. This sounds simple, but its structural importance is substantial. When risk intensity rises, the system does not merely become more vulnerable in principle. It begins consuming its survival interval more rapidly in practice. Obligations become more difficult to sequence, response inefficiencies rise, stabilizing actions draw more heavily on available funds, and delayed or impaired inflows reduce offsetting support. The result is that liquidity translates into fewer units of usable time. The same nominal quantity buys less survival duration under higher-risk conditions than under lower-risk ones.

This is the central interaction: liquidity determines how much time exists, and risk determines how quickly that time is used. Because of this, survival cannot be assessed by looking at liquidity alone. It must be assessed by examining the depletion slope under current conditions. Risk changes the slope of time loss. It alters not just the endpoint at which liquidity is exhausted, but the pace at which the system moves toward that endpoint. Risk therefore determines how quickly time is consumed.

The depletion rate is the speed at which liquidity is used up. Under calm conditions, depletion tends to be more predictable. Outflows are more stable, sequencing is more orderly, inefficiencies are lower, and the system can often estimate how quickly liquidity is likely to decline. Under stress, depletion becomes less stable and more dangerous. It accelerates, and often does so nonlinearly. This acceleration can occur even without a new external shock because instability within the structure changes how fast existing pressures consume the remaining buffer.

Several forces drive this acceleration. Obligations may intensify relative to available inflow. Inflow itself may weaken, become delayed, or become less reliable. Forced adjustments may require immediate spending or bridging that increases short-term burn. Operational inefficiencies may rise under pressure as the system reallocates resources in less efficient ways to preserve continuity. Each of these increases the rate at which liquidity is consumed. More importantly, they can reinforce one another, so the depletion rate does not simply rise by a fixed increment. It can steepen as instability deepens.

This establishes the distinction between linear consumption and accelerated consumption. Linear consumption assumes a relatively stable burn pattern across time. Accelerated consumption describes a state in which each interval consumes liquidity faster than the previous one because the system is deteriorating or becoming more expensive to sustain under stress. In such a condition, runway collapses faster than a constant-rate model would predict. The system may appear to have more remaining time than it actually does because nominal liquidity is being evaluated against outdated burn assumptions.

The structural consequence is that the system may lose time faster than expected even without further external deterioration. Once instability is active, internal conditions can increase the depletion rate on their own. This is why depletion rate is more important than the liquidity balance viewed in isolation. The system does not fail because liquidity reaches zero in a purely mechanical sense. It fails because the rate of decline in available survival time overtakes the pace at which continuity can be maintained or stability restored. Depletion rate determines how quickly runway collapses.

Liquidity decline also contracts the stability margin. Within the existing structure, stability margin refers to the remaining tolerance before instability becomes irreversible or unmanageable. Liquidity does not merely support operations in a static way. It preserves this margin by buying time within which disruption can still be absorbed, delayed, or redirected. As liquidity falls, the remaining interval during which the system can respond narrows, and the system becomes more sensitive to additional variation.

This introduces the distinction between capacity presence and remaining margin. Capacity presence asks whether the system still possesses resources. Remaining margin asks how much of the usable distance between current operation and destabilizing consequence is left. A system may still have liquidity in nominal terms while already having very little true stability margin because that liquidity no longer supports much temporal flexibility. Less liquidity means less time to absorb disruption, less time to sequence responses, and less time for any adjustment to matter before thresholds are engaged more fully.

This matters because liquidity preserves more than duration. It preserves optionality inside duration. When liquidity is ample, the system not only has longer runway but also more tolerance for modest error, delay, and variation inside that runway. When liquidity contracts, the system's remaining time becomes more rigid. The same number of days or weeks may exist on paper, but far less flexibility exists inside them. This is why stability declines not only because resources fall, but because margin disappears. The temporal interval loses protective depth as liquidity shrinks.

In this sense, liquidity is the primary survival variable. Many conditions influence whether a system is well-structured or poorly structured, but liquidity determines whether those conditions can be managed across time once instability is active. Without liquidity, there is no interval in which correction, containment, or adjustment can occur. Without liquidity, delays cannot be bridged, obligations cannot be carried forward, and operating continuity cannot be preserved while deeper responses take effect. Liquidity sits upstream of recovery, adjustment, and containment because each of those processes requires time, and liquidity is what purchases time.

This creates the distinction between structural strength and survivability duration. A system may be structurally sound in many respects and still fail if liquidity is insufficient to bridge the period in which that structural soundness would otherwise matter. Conversely, a system with weaknesses can survive longer if liquidity extends the period over which those weaknesses must be managed. This does not mean liquidity overrides structure. It means liquidity governs whether structure has time to operate. A structurally strong system can still fail if time runs out first. A weaker system can remain viable longer if liquidity extends the runway far enough to keep failure from arriving immediately.

The implication is that liquidity governs whether recovery remains possible in practical terms. Recovery cannot occur inside zero time. Adjustment cannot occur after continuity has already broken irreversibly. Containment cannot succeed if the interval in which it could work has already been consumed. Liquidity is therefore the variable that determines whether the system's remaining strengths still have operational value. It converts structural possibility into temporal feasibility.

As liquidity declines, effective response windows shrink. This is the temporal compression effect expressed through the liquidity channel. The distinction here is between absolute time and usable time. Absolute time continues to pass normally, but usable time contracts because fewer intervals remain in which the system can recognize, process, and respond to worsening conditions before consequences escalate. Liquidity depletion reduces not just duration, but decision space within that duration. This is the central temporal consequence of runway loss.

Less liquidity means less time between disruption and consequence. It also means less room for mis-sequencing, less tolerance for delayed response, and less ability to let a problem remain localized while deciding how to address it. The result is that time-to-failure compression intensifies as liquidity falls. Even if no new shock arrives, the same continuing pressure becomes more dangerous because the system now has fewer intervals left in which to do anything about it. Liquidity loss therefore accelerates failure not merely by reducing total survivability, but by narrowing the practical windows for intervention inside that survivability.

Runway itself behaves nonlinearly under stress. It does not decline as a smooth, evenly sloped line. Early in a stress sequence, runway may shrink gradually while the system still retains significant margin and the depletion rate remains relatively contained. In the middle stage, contraction accelerates as burn rises, flexibility narrows, and sensitivity increases. In the late stage, the remaining runway often collapses very quickly because the last usable liquidity is being consumed in a system that has little margin left and few stabilizing options still available.

This creates the distinction between apparent runway and actual remaining survival time. Apparent runway is what a simple, static calculation suggests based on current liquidity and an assumed ordinary burn rate. Actual remaining survival time is what the system can truly sustain under current or worsening depletion conditions. The difference widens under stress because depletion is accelerating and the system's burn characteristics are changing as it becomes more unstable. The last portion of runway disappears faster than the first because the system is spending from a smaller base, under higher pressure, with less flexibility and less capacity to moderate burn.

This nonlinearity is one of the most dangerous aspects of liquidity interaction. Systems often appear to have meaningful remaining runway when they still possess visible liquidity, yet the speed at which that remaining runway is being consumed may have already shifted into a more dangerous regime. What seems like sufficient time under a linear model can prove insufficient under actual stress conditions because the depletion slope steepens as the system deteriorates. Runway therefore cannot be understood as a simple countdown. It is a dynamic interval whose final stages contract more sharply than its earlier ones.

Liquidity also interacts with the underlying structure already established across prior chapters. Concentration increases liquidity sensitivity because more continuity depends on fewer supported points, so depletion at one channel has broader consequence. Correlation accelerates simultaneous depletion because multiple pressures draw on the same remaining liquidity at once. Coupling spreads liquidity pressure across domains, causing what begins as a local funding issue to become wider operating strain. Proximity to critical limits amplifies the consequence of each additional unit of depletion because less time remains before structural boundaries become active. These interactions need not be restated in full. What matters here is that structure determines depletion pattern, while liquidity determines the timeline along which that pattern becomes fatal.

This clarifies the role of liquidity as the medium through which structural weakness becomes time-bound failure. Weaknesses may exist in concentration, correlation, coupling, or other established properties, but they do not translate into breakdown until the runway available to manage them is consumed. Liquidity gives those weaknesses a temporal expression. It tells the system how long its structure can continue functioning under present pressure. Once the answer becomes "not long enough," structural weakness becomes operational failure.

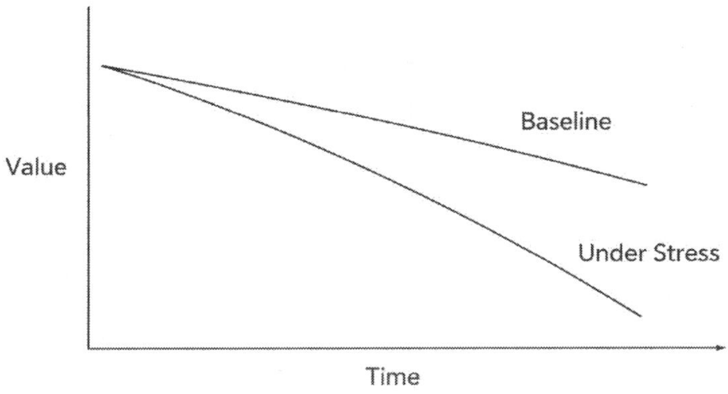

[Figure 10: Risk vs Runway Depletion]

The figure makes this visible. Along the horizontal axis, time progresses. Along the vertical axis, remaining runway declines. In a low-risk environment, the slope is gradual. Liquidity is still being consumed, but the depletion rate remains modest enough that runway declines in a relatively controlled manner. In a high-risk environment, the slope is steeper and increasingly so. The same nominal starting runway disappears much faster because risk changes the rate of time loss. The critical point is not merely that high-risk systems reach zero sooner. It is that the curve itself changes. Risk alters the slope of depletion, making the time interval collapse more rapidly as pressure intensifies.

This figure is useful because it shifts attention from endpoint to gradient. The question is not only how much runway remains at the beginning of the observation period. It is how sharply the runway is declining under current conditions. A system with moderate runway and low depletion intensity may remain viable longer than a system with greater nominal runway but a steep depletion curve. The slope is therefore structurally more informative than the raw amount. It shows how risk transforms liquidity from a stock into a wasting interval.

The mechanism resolves into a simple but consequential structure. Systems do not fail only because resources are insufficient in the abstract. They fail because time runs out before stability can be restored. Liquidity is time. Risk is the rate at which that time is consumed. Runway is the remaining survival interval available under current conditions. Survival depends simultaneously on how much time remains and how quickly that time is being depleted. The system's fate is therefore not determined by resources alone, but by whether those resources can sustain continuity for long enough to prevent instability from becoming terminal.

Failure is not only the result of insufficient resources, but of insufficient time to use them.

The Income Interaction Mechanism

The Income Interaction Mechanism defines income not as a fixed base of support, but as a variable inflow whose behavior changes with conditions and whose stability cannot be separated from the stability of the system it supports. Income is often treated as an external constant: a stream assumed to arrive with enough regularity that the rest of the structure can be built around it. Mechanically, that assumption is weak. Income varies in timing, magnitude, and reliability. It is contingent rather than guaranteed. More importantly, it is state-dependent. As conditions deteriorate, income can become less reliable. As income becomes less reliable, conditions can deteriorate further. The mechanism therefore begins with a rejection of the fixed-base model. Income is not only an input into stability. It is also a variable shaped by the system's exposure and condition.

This distinction separates nominal income from reliable income. Nominal income describes the amount that appears in ordinary reporting across some interval. Reliable income describes the portion of inflow that persists with sufficient continuity under pressure to sustain obligations, operations, and timing requirements when conditions worsen. The difference between the two is not marginal. A system can appear well supported in nominal terms while being structurally exposed because the income base on which continuity depends is conditional, concentrated, or timing-sensitive. Average level is therefore a weak stability measure. What matters is continuity under strain. Income must be evaluated by whether it continues functioning when the system is stressed, not by whether it looked sufficient during calm intervals.

This makes income a conditional stream rather than a neutral foundation. It can vary by amount without warning, arrive irregularly relative to demand, or weaken precisely when the rest of the structure most needs reinforcement. These variations do not need to be extreme in order to matter. A system built on narrow timing tolerances, thin margins, and heavy reliance on continuous inflow can convert even modest inconsistency into meaningful structural pressure. Stability assumptions that treat income as fixed therefore embed unacknowledged exposure. They assign continuity obligations to a variable input while modeling it as though it were stable. The result is a structure that appears balanced only while the income stream behaves more reliably than its actual design warrants.

Income variability creates instability even in the absence of a discrete external shock because it alters the internal conditions under which continuity must be maintained. Variation in inflow timing, amount, or dependability disrupts the relationship between support and demand. This does not require large declines. Small inconsistencies can matter because they accumulate into tighter timing windows, greater reliance on buffers, and narrower room for sequencing error. A system can therefore become more fragile without any dramatic collapse in income level if the reliability of that income begins to weaken.

The key distinction here is between level of income and predictability of income. Two systems with similar average inflow can behave very differently if one receives income in a consistent and dependable pattern while the other receives it with variable timing or irregular continuity. Predictability stabilizes because it allows the rest of the structure to align around a known support interval. Variability destabilizes because it widens the gap between what is expected and what is actually available when needed. The average amount may remain unchanged while the structural burden of maintaining continuity rises sharply.

This is why income instability acts as an internal source of risk. It is not only a background fluctuation to be noted after the fact. It changes the behavior of the whole system by increasing reliance on reserves, reducing timing slack, and forcing more of the structure into compressed response modes. When income becomes less predictable, buffers are drawn more frequently, sequencing becomes more rigid, and margin is consumed faster. These pressures do not wait for a dramatic break. They begin operating as soon as variability becomes large enough to interfere with continuity assumptions. Income instability therefore accelerates the compression of time and margin from inside the system itself.

When income is disrupted more severely, the consequences intensify because the system loses its primary replenishment mechanism. Other forms of strain become more dangerous when inflow is weakened because the structure is no longer replacing what it is consuming at the rate assumed by normal operation. Liquidity declines faster. Obligations become harder to sequence and sustain. Timing mismatches that would have been temporary under normal inflow begin extending across intervals. Income disruption therefore does not remain local to the inflow channel. It propagates through the rest of the structure by reducing the system's capacity to replenish what pressure is already consuming.

This creates the distinction between temporary disruption and structural destabilization. A temporary disruption is a short-lived interruption whose effects remain contained because the rest of the system can absorb the gap. Structural destabilization begins when the income disruption changes the rate at which other pressures become dangerous. The system moves from managing a shortfall to reorganizing itself around a diminished replenishment base. At that point, the disruption is no longer just an income event. It is a multiplier of every other pressure that depends on continued inflow.

The reason is straightforward. Income is the primary route through which many systems restore usable capacity across time. When that route weakens, depletion accelerates even if the external environment does not worsen further. The slope of decline steepens because the system is still operating under obligations, still consuming liquidity, and still requiring timing coordination, but it is doing so with less replenishment. This is why loss of inflow increases the consequence of all other pressures. The same obligations become more dangerous. The same delays become more expensive. The same structural weaknesses become harder to manage because the supply of ongoing support has diminished.

The mechanism becomes more severe when the relationship between income and system condition becomes recursive. A feedback loop exists here because system state affects income, and income affects system state. Increased instability can reduce income reliability. Reduced income can then increase instability further. This loop does not require a new external shock at every stage. Once active, it can continue through the interaction between weakened inflow and worsening structure. What begins as one-directional pressure becomes recursive deterioration.

This distinction between one-directional impact and recursive interaction matters because it changes how disruption grows. In a one-directional model, income declines and the system absorbs the consequence as best it can. In a recursive model, the weakened system itself becomes part of the reason income continues to weaken. Reduced continuity can affect the persistence, timing, or reliability of income sources. That further weakening then feeds more strain back into the system. Linear disruption becomes compounding instability because the system is now participating in its own worsening through the income channel.

This recursive behavior can operate quietly at first. A moderate decline in reliability increases the need for stabilization effort. That effort consumes liquidity and narrows timing margin. The more compressed state then makes income continuity more vulnerable to subsequent interruption, delay, or inconsistency. A second round of inflow weakness arrives into a system already less able to absorb it. The consequence is not just additive decline. Each round weakens the base from which the next round must be managed. Feedback loops transform income instability from a background fluctuation into an active accelerator of structural pressure.

A more precise expression of this appears in dependency loops. A dependency loop exists when the system depends on income for continuity while income itself depends, at least in part, on the system's stability for persistence. This means income is not fully external to the structure. It is partially endogenous. Its continuity is influenced by the same system condition it is expected to support. As the system weakens, some income sources may degrade. As those sources degrade, the system weakens further. The relationship is circular rather than linear.

This is the difference between an independent input and a co-dependent input. An independent input remains largely unaffected by the system's changing condition. A co-dependent input deteriorates with the system because its own continuity is tied to the health, timing, access, or operating range of the structure receiving it. Many income streams are not wholly one or the other. They contain degrees of dependence that become more visible under stress. The importance of the mechanism lies in recognizing that income cannot always be modeled as untouched by the condition of the system it supports.

Dependency loops increase fragility because both sides of the relationship weaken together. The system depends on income, and income depends on the system's ability to remain functional enough to preserve that inflow's continuity. Once deterioration begins, the loop can tighten quickly. What appeared to be a support channel becomes part of the pressure architecture because its reliability declines as soon as the system needs it most. This does not make income internal in the sense of being fully controllable. It makes it partially coupled to system state, which is enough to change its behavior under strain.

Sensitivity determines how strongly these changes affect outcome. Income sensitivity is the degree to which system stability depends on continuity of inflow. In a highly sensitive system, small changes in income timing, reliability, or amount produce large effects because too much of the structure relies on uninterrupted inflow. In a less sensitive system, similar income variation produces smaller effects because other buffers, pathways, or supports reduce the burden carried by the income channel. Sensitivity is therefore not about whether income matters. It is about how much system outcome changes when income continuity weakens.

This establishes the distinction between income presence and income dependence. A system may have substantial income and still be highly fragile if continuity depends tightly on that income arriving in precise form and sequence. Another system may have more modest income and greater tolerance if continuity is less tightly tied to any single stream or interval. Sensitivity increases with concentrated income sources, narrow timing tolerance, and low margin. It declines when continuity is less dependent on uninterrupted performance of any one inflow channel.

The consequence is that fragility rises when system outcome is tightly linked to income continuity. If continuity requires the same inflow to arrive predictably and on time in order for obligations, operations, and timing coordination to function, then small disturbances in income become disproportionately important. Stability improves when dependence on any single income stream is reduced because failure in one stream then carries less consequence for the whole structure. This point does not require full restatement of earlier distribution logic. Here it serves to specify how income sensitivity mediates the strength of the interaction between inflow instability and system deterioration.

Income also interacts directly with liquidity by determining how quickly time is restored once it has begun to be consumed. Inflow replenishes liquidity. Liquidity, in turn, preserves time. When income weakens, replenishment slows or stops, and depletion accelerates. The distinction here is between inflow and available time. Income is the channel through which time is replenished. Liquidity is the stock through which time is held. If income becomes unstable, the system loses not only money in the narrow sense, but the ability to restore the interval in which it can continue operating.

This relationship is structurally upstream. Income determines how fast time is rebuilt after usage. Liquidity determines how long that time lasts once currently available. When income is stable, liquidity can be replenished and runway can recover or at least stabilize. When income is unstable, effective runway shortens because the system keeps consuming time without restoring it at the rate assumed by normal operation. Income instability therefore shortens effective runway even before absolute liquidity appears critically low, because the rate of replenishment has already deteriorated.

The temporal effects of income instability extend beyond depletion rate into sequencing and coordination. Income variability introduces timing uncertainty. When inflow arrives irregularly, the structure loses a dependable reference point around which obligations, operational cycles, and adaptive responses can be sequenced. Stable timing supports orderly coordination because components can be arranged around a known replenishment rhythm. Irregular timing weakens that rhythm and forces multiple demands into tighter or less predictable intervals.

This creates the distinction between stable timing and irregular timing. Stable timing preserves temporal separation between pressures. Irregular timing reduces that separation. When inflow becomes less predictable, coordination difficulty rises because fewer components can rely on orderly sequencing. The system experiences more overlap between demands, more compression of usable response windows, and greater difficulty keeping one pressure from colliding with another. The problem is not merely that income is delayed or variable. It is that the uncertainty in timing reorganizes the rest of the system into a more compressed, less forgiving state.

Income instability therefore reduces temporal separation between pressures. Problems that could have remained distinct under predictable inflow start arriving inside the same operating interval because replenishment no longer occurs when expected. This makes the system harder to coordinate and easier to destabilize, even if the total amount of income across a broader period has not yet declined dramatically. Timing uncertainty acts as a transmission amplifier because it shrinks the windows in which otherwise separate adjustments could have been made sequentially.

A final distinction must be drawn between apparent income stability and structural income stability. Apparent stability exists when income appears consistent under calm conditions. Structural stability exists when income remains reliable under stress. The difference is decisive because calm conditions can conceal concentration, shared dependencies, and coupling between income continuity and broader system state. An income stream may look stable simply because the conditions that would expose its fragility have not yet been activated.

Observed consistency is therefore not enough. Income that has not been tested under adverse conditions may appear safer than it is. If its stability depends on calm environments, narrow dependency channels, or system conditions that deteriorate under pressure, then its apparent consistency is conditional rather than structural. Stability based on untested income assumptions is fragile because it assigns too much continuity to a stream whose true behavior under strain remains unknown or misunderstood.

This is why income must be evaluated according to stress reliability rather than calm-state appearance. A stream that looks regular when margins are wide and pressures are low may still become unstable when continuity is most needed. The system that treats observed consistency as proof of structural reliability is vulnerable because it mistakes performance in easy conditions for durability in hard ones. Structural income stability exists only where continuity persists when the system is under pressure, not merely where inflow appears smooth when nothing is testing it.

The mechanism resolves into a clear structural conclusion. Income is not a passive input that simply supports the system from outside. It is an active participant in system stability. Variability introduces instability even without large shocks. Disruption amplifies existing pressure by weakening the primary replenishment mechanism. Feedback loops make the relationship recursive by allowing system weakness to degrade income and income weakness to deepen system weakness. Dependency loops bind inflow to system condition. Timing instability compresses coordination and reduces effective runway. What results is not merely reduced income, but compounded risk.

Risk therefore increases not only through external shocks, but through income interaction itself. The system does not need an entirely new disturbance for instability to deepen. Income can become a channel through which existing pressure intensifies and sustains itself. That is the core of the mechanism: inflow is variable, condition-sensitive, and capable of feeding deterioration back into the system that depends on it.

Income does not merely support the system—it can also accelerate its instability when its continuity is disrupted.

The Expense Interaction Mechanism

The Expense Interaction Mechanism defines expenses not as passive outflows, but as structural commitments that shape how much tolerance remains when conditions change. Once established, expenses do not simply record what a system happens to spend. They define required claims on capacity. They determine how much outflow must continue, when it must occur, and how much baseline load the system must carry before any optional activity, adaptive action, or recovery process can begin. In that sense, expenses are not downstream artifacts of operation. They are pre-committed demands embedded into the structure itself.

This distinction is essential because it separates variable outflow from committed outflow. Variable outflows can contract, shift, or disappear with relatively limited structural consequence. Committed outflows remain due regardless of system condition. They form the minimum operating threshold that the system must satisfy in order to preserve continuity. Once these commitments exist, they cease to function as discretionary uses of resources and begin functioning as fixed claims on timing, liquidity, and ongoing support. The system is therefore constrained less by what it can choose to spend and more by what it must continue to spend.

Expenses define the required continuity level of the structure. They encode assumptions about the ongoing availability of inflow, timing precision, and liquidity access. A system with a high committed expense base is not merely one with a high spending profile. It is one that has elevated the minimum conditions required for continued operation. This means that expense structure determines how much deviation the system can tolerate before strain becomes destabilizing. The more of total outflow is committed in advance, the smaller the interval between normal operation and active pressure.

Rigidity is the key property that converts expenses from manageable load into structural vulnerability. Expense rigidity refers to the degree to which commitments cannot be reduced, delayed, or restructured within the timeframe required by changing conditions. This is independent of nominal size. A large expense that can be adjusted quickly may be less destabilizing than a smaller expense that cannot move at all. Rigidity is therefore a structural property of the expense, not simply a measure of magnitude. It describes how much adaptive capacity remains available once pressure begins.

This distinction between expense magnitude and expense flexibility is central. Systems often focus on the size of the cost base because it is easily visible, but visibility does not reveal how the structure behaves under stress. A smaller but inflexible obligation may create more acute pressure than a larger but adjustable one because the former continues to demand full support precisely when support conditions weaken. Flexibility, not size alone, determines whether the system can alter its demand profile quickly enough to remain within tolerable bounds. Survivability is therefore shaped more by the adjustability of load than by its nominal total in isolation.

Rigidity increases sensitivity because it reduces the number of available response pathways. When expenses cannot be reduced, delayed, or restructured, the system has fewer ways to align outflow with changing inflow and shrinking liquidity. This does not require a dramatic deterioration in external conditions. Even modest disruption becomes more dangerous when commitments remain fixed and unresponsive. The structure becomes more brittle because every change in conditions must now be absorbed by a narrower set of remaining variables. Risk increases when expenses cannot adjust to changing conditions because the system is forced to maintain the same demand profile even as its support profile weakens.

Fixed costs are the clearest expression of this interaction. Fixed expenses continue regardless of system condition. They do not wait for income to recover, for liquidity to replenish, or for timing pressure to ease. When inflow weakens, fixed costs remain constant, and the imbalance becomes active immediately. This is what makes fixed costs such strong accelerators of instability. They translate any variation in support into direct structural strain because they preserve the same outflow requirement while the system's ability to meet that requirement changes.

The distinction here is between adjustable and non-adjustable cost structures. In an adjustable structure, support deterioration can be partially matched by a change in load. In a non-adjustable structure, support deterioration meets unchanged demand. The result is that variability in income or liquidity becomes immediately consequential. Fixed costs do not create instability on their own in every case, but they remove the system's ability to reduce baseline pressure when support weakens. They therefore convert support variability into active imbalance faster than adjustable costs do.

This is why fixed costs steepen the depletion curve. Once inflow weakens, the system continues to spend at the same committed rate, drawing more heavily on reserves, shortening runway, and reducing the time available for stabilization. The more rigid the cost base, the faster instability progresses under disruption because the system cannot slow its own rate of resource consumption. It is compelled to continue funding obligations at a level that no longer matches current support conditions. Fixed costs do not merely coexist with instability. They intensify it by preserving demand while capacity erodes.

The deeper consequence is reduced adaptability under stress. Adaptation requires some ability to lower load, reallocate resources, or delay commitments long enough to restore alignment. Rigid expenses suppress all three. If baseline demand cannot be reduced, then the system cannot create additional margin from the outflow side. If commitments cannot be re-sequenced, then timing flexibility is reduced. If resources cannot be redirected because fixed expenses absorb them first, then alternative responses lose viability. The structure is constrained not because response effort is absent, but because the commitments themselves have already consumed much of the room in which response could occur.

This establishes the distinction between an adaptive system and a constrained system. An adaptive system preserves the ability to change its demand profile when support conditions shift. A constrained system must maintain much of its existing demand even when the environment no longer supports it cleanly. Under stress, the constrained system may still take operational actions, but those actions occur inside a structure whose commitments have already fixed much of the relevant load. The result is that operational motion continues while structural flexibility remains low. The system can still act, but it cannot change the aspects of itself that most need changing.

This is why systems fail not only from pressure, but from inability to adjust to pressure. A rigid expense base transforms disruption from a manageable mismatch into a narrowing of viable options. The system cannot lower baseline demand, cannot meaningfully widen margin from the expense side, and cannot easily extend its response interval. The burden of adaptation then falls disproportionately on liquidity, timing precision, or whatever small portion of the structure remains flexible. That concentration of adaptive burden is itself destabilizing, because it forces too much response work into too few remaining channels.

One of the clearest results of this is compression of the survivability window. The survivability window is the interval between onset of disruption and failure. Resources matter within this interval, but the relevant variable is not resource size alone. It is the rate at which those resources are consumed. Rigid expenses maintain constant outflow even when support weakens, which means depletion continues at a pace that the system can no longer comfortably sustain. The higher the fixed load, the less time remains before available resources are exhausted or operational limits are reached.

This creates the distinction between time determined by resources and time determined by burn rate. A system may appear to possess enough resources to last for a meaningful period, but if rigid expenses force those resources to be consumed quickly, the effective survivability window is short. Conversely, a system with fewer total resources but lower fixed outflow may preserve a longer interval because the rate of consumption is lower. Survivability is governed by rate of consumption, not just total capacity. This is especially important under stress, because fixed obligations can continue draining the structure even without any increase in external pressure.

The internal outflow pressure of rigid expenses therefore shortens time-to-failure on its own. Even if no new shock arrives, continued fixed demand keeps converting stored capacity into spent capacity. This is why fixed obligations turn time into a rapidly diminishing resource. The system is not only spending money. It is spending survivability. Each interval of unchanged outflow under weakened support consumes another portion of the time that might otherwise have been available for stabilization. Rigidity makes that interval shrink faster because it prevents the system from slowing the pace at which time is being burned.

This relationship becomes even clearer when expenses are considered in direct interaction with liquidity. Expenses draw from liquidity, and liquidity defines available time. A highly predictable expense schedule can create the appearance of order, but predictability is not the same as safety when the outflow is inflexible. The system may know when obligations are coming, yet still be highly vulnerable if those obligations cannot adjust to changing support conditions. Predictable outflow is only stabilizing when it is also structurally manageable. If it is rigid, then predictability merely clarifies the pace at which the system is losing time.

This is the distinction between predictable and adjustable. Predictability helps sequencing under calm conditions. Adjustability matters under stress. A rigid expense may be fully predictable and still destabilizing because it provides no room to respond when inflow weakens or timing misaligns. In such a case, the expense structure defines the slope of liquidity depletion. It determines how quickly available time is consumed because each committed outflow removes another portion of usable runway regardless of whether the rest of the system has regained balance.

Expense density adds another layer of structural load. Density refers to the concentration of expenses within particular time windows, obligations, or dependencies. Even moderate total expenses can destabilize a system if they are clustered tightly or synchronized poorly. Structural pressure is shaped not only by how much must be paid, but by when it must be paid and how many demands converge in the same interval. Costs that are manageable in aggregate may still create acute stress if they are concentrated into narrow periods where liquidity, timing, and sequencing must all perform simultaneously.

This establishes the distinction between total cost and timing distribution of cost. Aggregate outflow across a month, quarter, or year may look sustainable, yet the actual operating burden may be highly uneven if commitments cluster. High density creates pressure spikes, forcing the system to meet several demands at once instead of distributing them across recoverable intervals. This raises coordination requirements because more obligations must be aligned with the same limited set of support channels. Expense clustering therefore increases sensitivity to disruption. A delay or shortfall that would have been manageable in a more dispersed structure becomes more dangerous when dense outflow windows already exist.

The destabilizing effect of density does not depend on extreme cost levels. It depends on synchronization. A system can be strained by moderate expenses if too many of them align inside the same narrow interval or depend on the same support event. This is why structural pressure is determined by alignment and timing, not only by total outflow. Density reduces the number of intervals in which the system can recover between commitments. It narrows the spacing that would otherwise help localize strain. Once disruption appears, clustered expenses magnify its consequence because there is less time and less slack between demands.

Expenses also encode assumptions about system continuity. Many commitments are viable only under the condition that income remains continuous, liquidity remains available, and timing remains orderly. When those assumptions hold, expenses appear neutral. They are simply part of the system's ordinary operating pattern. When those assumptions fail, the same expenses become destabilizing because they continue to demand fulfillment from a structure whose support conditions have changed. Expenses are therefore not independent of the system. They are dependent claims on continuity.

This creates the distinction between supported expenses and unsupported expenses. Supported expenses are commitments that remain aligned with actual support conditions. Unsupported expenses are commitments whose assumed support no longer exists in the required form, timing, or volume. The expense itself may not have changed, but its relationship to the system has. What was once sustainable now becomes destabilizing because the underlying conditions that made it sustainable have weakened or disappeared. Fragility increases when expenses rely on conditions that may not hold, because the structure has encoded those conditions into ongoing demand.

This is one of the most important hidden properties of expense structure. Expenses are not passive records of prior choices. They are ongoing claims that presuppose continuity in other parts of the system. If income weakens, if liquidity tightens, if timing becomes irregular, or if access to support narrows, the expense base does not automatically adapt. Instead, it continues to impose the same demands, revealing how much of the structure depended on conditions that were never guaranteed. Expenses therefore expose dependency by turning assumptions about continuity into concrete, recurring obligations.

A final distinction must be drawn between operational control and structural control. Systems may retain considerable operational control in the day-to-day sense. They can shift priorities, rearrange tasks, make local decisions, or manage small adjustments. But these capacities do not necessarily imply structural control if the expense base itself remains rigid. Under stress, operational responsiveness often proves insufficient because the main source of pressure is not lack of movement at the surface. It is the fixed nature of the commitments beneath it. The system can still act while lacking the ability to alter the deeper structure that determines how much outflow must continue.

This distinction matters because it explains why control can appear present while stability deteriorates. The system continues making decisions, but those decisions occur inside a fixed expense architecture that has already committed much of the available capacity. Operational choices then affect only the narrow margin that remains outside the expense base. Structural rigidity dominates outcome because it defines the size of baseline demand, the flexibility of timing, and the rate at which support is consumed. The ability to act is therefore not the same as the ability to change the conditions that matter most.

This is why stability depends more on structural flexibility than on operational responsiveness. A system with high day-to-day control but low structural flexibility remains vulnerable because the commitments governing its burn rate and minimum load cannot move enough under stress. Control is limited when structure is fixed. The system may respond intelligently and continuously, yet still be overpowered by the unyielding demands embedded in its expense base. Structural flexibility determines whether operational effort has enough room to matter. Without it, response remains active but structurally constrained.

The mechanism resolves into a clear conclusion. Expenses define baseline demand. Rigidity limits adaptability. Fixed costs accelerate depletion. Timing density increases pressure. Continuity assumptions embedded in expenses create exposure when support conditions weaken. Together, these conditions narrow system tolerance by preserving demand even as capacity contracts. The system does not become fragile simply because it has expenses. It becomes fragile when those expenses are rigid enough, dense enough, and dependent enough on uninterrupted support that they cannot adjust when conditions change.

Rigidity reduces system tolerance because it preserves load while removing adaptive space. The more fixed the cost base, the more quickly pressure converts into instability, the less time remains for response, and the harder it becomes to align outflow with altered inflow and liquidity conditions. Survivability is therefore constrained not only by how much support the system has, but by how much of its demand can still move under stress.

Expenses do not merely reflect system activity—they determine how much strain the system can endure before stability gives way.

The Continuity of Controlled Stability

The Continuity of Controlled Stability defines stability as a continuous condition of managed exposure rather than a fixed state achieved once and then preserved passively. Stability does not emerge because risk has been eliminated, variability has been reduced to zero, or the system has been optimized into permanence. It exists when disruption remains contained within tolerable bounds, when absorptive depth remains sufficient relative to active pressure, when response time and flexibility are preserved, and when local strain is prevented from expanding into collapse. This condition is never final. It depends on whether the structure continues to hold disruption inside the range the system can survive.

This requires a redefinition of stability itself. Stability is not the absence of risk. It is not the disappearance of disturbance. It is not a state in which no variability enters the system. Systems remain exposed continuously. Variation is not an exception layered onto an otherwise frictionless structure. It is part of the environment in which the structure operates. Stability therefore cannot be defined as eliminated risk. It must be defined as contained risk. The relevant question is not whether disruption exists, but whether disruption remains inside the structural range where it can be absorbed without changing the system's operating regime.

The distinction between eliminated risk and contained risk is therefore decisive. Eliminated risk would imply a system no longer subject to variation, dependency stress, timing pressure, or uncertainty. Such a condition is not structurally available. Contained risk means the system remains exposed, but that exposure is bounded by sufficient depth, limitation, and continuity support that incoming disturbance does not exceed absorbable range. The structure remains vulnerable in principle, yet viable in practice, because failure modes are constrained before they become dominant. Stability exists not because the system has escaped uncertainty, but because it continues functioning inside limits that uncertainty has not yet breached.

This makes stability a condition of containment rather than protection in an absolute sense. The system is still subject to interruption, mismatch, pressure, and loss. What distinguishes stable operation is that these conditions do not propagate beyond the range the system can absorb. A disruption may enter, but it does not reorganize the system into instability. It remains local enough, limited enough, and slow enough that continuity persists. The system therefore remains exposed, but not destabilized. That is the governing distinction on which the chapter rests.

Because exposure remains continuous, stability depends on continuous exposure management. Exposure is not episodic. It does not come into existence only when visible disruption arrives. It persists as a standing condition in the architecture of the system, shaped by how dependency, timing, capacity, and limitation are arranged at any given point. This means there is no stable endpoint at which exposure disappears and management is no longer necessary. Exposure can be redistributed, limited, buffered, or contained. It cannot be made structurally irrelevant across all conditions.

The relevant contrast here is between static safety and dynamic management. Static safety would imply that the system has reached a condition in which it no longer requires active structural regulation because its exposure has effectively been neutralized. Dynamic management recognizes that exposure continues to exist even when it is not visible in outcomes. The system remains within stable bounds only while exposure is being monitored, distributed, limited, and absorbed in a way that preserves continuity. Stability is therefore not a one-time correction. It is the maintained consequence of ongoing structural adjustment.

This follows directly from the fact that accumulation is continuous. Pressure can build beneath a calm surface, concentration can increase during uninterrupted periods, and dependency can become more consequential precisely when nothing visibly breaks. If exposure continues accumulating in ordinary time, then control must also continue in ordinary time. Stability cannot be maintained through episodic correction alone because the conditions that undermine it are not episodic. They persist and shift whether or not a visible event has occurred. Stability is thus maintained through ongoing regulation of exposure, not by assuming that the absence of immediate disruption implies enduring safety.

That leads to the distinction between reactive control and structural control. Reactive control refers to responses applied after disruption has already become visible. Structural control refers to the prior configuration that determines whether disruption can escalate once it arrives. Both may exist within a system, but they do not carry equal weight. Under compressed conditions, reactive capacity shrinks because the time available to recognize, sequence, and materially alter the consequences of disruption narrows rapidly once transmission is underway. Structural control operates earlier. It shapes what disruption is able to become before reactive intervention is even relevant.

The distinction is therefore between response and configuration. Response can still matter, but its effectiveness is conditional on what configuration has preserved in advance. If the structure has retained limitation, margin, redundancy, layered absorption, and distributed dependency, then disruption can arrive into a system that still possesses usable room for response. If those conditions are absent, reaction occurs inside a narrowing interval where the structure has already pre-committed too much of the outcome. Stability is therefore governed by structure more than by reaction. Response takes place inside the conditions that structure has already defined.

This is especially important because reactive control is often overestimated during calm periods. Systems may infer from prior successful responses that reaction itself is the governing source of stability. But many successful responses owe their success to structural room that had not yet been fully consumed. Once propagation begins and response windows compress, that room shrinks quickly. The practical meaning is clear: control must exist before disruption, not be expected to arise after it. The system remains stable because escalation paths were constrained in advance, not because reaction can always outrun structural deterioration once it has begun.

Risk persists across time even when outcomes do not visibly reflect it. This is one of the most important features of controlled stability. Risk does not disappear between events. It remains present as structural exposure, encoded in the arrangement of obligations, dependencies, timing assumptions, and support layers. Calm periods reveal only that current conditions have not activated the full consequence of that exposure. They do not demonstrate that the exposure is absent. The difference between observed stability and structural exposure therefore remains active at all times.

This distinction matters because calm periods are easily misread as proof of low risk. In reality, calm conceals as much as it confirms. Structural exposure may persist unchanged or even intensify beneath a stable outcome stream because the conditions required to reveal it have not yet been triggered. The system continues appearing stable while the underlying architecture may be becoming narrower, denser, or more timing-sensitive. This means that absence of visible disruption does not imply absence of risk. It implies only that current conditions remain inside the range where risk is not yet visibly expressing itself.

The implication is that risk is continuous even when outcomes are not. A system may experience long periods without overt instability while still carrying meaningful exposure. Controlled stability depends on preserving the capacity to govern that exposure during calm periods, not only on reacting when outcomes turn negative. If risk is treated as event-based, stability will be treated as something confirmed by the lack of recent disruption. If risk is treated as structural, stability becomes a condition that must be maintained even while outcomes appear orderly. The second interpretation is the one that aligns with the mechanics established throughout the book.

Stability must also be understood as a bounded condition. It is not binary in the simplistic sense of either fully present or fully absent. Nor is it a continuous function that deteriorates smoothly without regime change. Stability exists within structural limits. Inside those limits, variation remains absorbable and continuity can be preserved. Outside those limits, system behavior changes. The system may still function in some reduced sense, but it is no longer operating under the same rules of contained disturbance. It has crossed into a different state.

This creates the distinction between continuous function and bounded regime. A system may still be active while already moving outside stable bounds, just as it may look normal while nearing them. The key issue is not visible activity alone. It is position relative to the limits that determine whether disruption remains local or becomes transformative. Stability is preserved by staying within those bounds, not by avoiding all stress. Stress can exist continuously without destabilizing the system so long as it remains inside the range where containment, absorption, and response time are still sufficient.

Once those bounds are crossed, the consequences are not merely larger versions of ordinary strain. The system enters a different mode of behavior in which compression, transmission, and depletion begin to dominate. This is why boundedness matters more than calm appearance. A system can remain under pressure and still be stable if that pressure is bounded. It can look orderly and still be unstable in structural terms if it is operating too near the limits that define regime change. The maintenance of controlled stability therefore depends on preserving position relative to limits, not on mistaking the absence of visible disorder for proof that those limits are remote.

All of the major structural conditions established earlier contribute to this bounded stability, but none does so alone. Concentration increases consequence per failure by assigning too much continuity to too few points. Correlation aligns stress across components under adverse conditions. Hidden coupling links components beneath surface separation, making simultaneous strain more likely than calm-state observation suggests. Thresholds define the boundaries at which operating behavior changes. Cascade transmits local failure through those pre-existing connections. Time compression reduces usable response intervals once instability becomes active. Recovery constraints limit how much restoration remains feasible after damage has been imposed. Absorptive capacity determines how much variation can be contained before transmission begins. Downside limitation caps how large consequences can become. Redundancy and layering preserve continuity by introducing substitution and staged defense. Liquidity determines how much time the system has left under active strain. Income and expense interactions govern the durability and rigidity of inflow and outflow support.

The relevant point here is not to reopen each mechanism in full, but to recognize that stability emerges from their alignment rather than from any one of them in isolation. No single mechanism governs outcome independently. A system may be strong on one dimension and weak on another, with the resulting behavior determined by how those structural conditions interact in sequence. Stability is therefore not the product of one superior feature. It is the maintained condition that exists when the major properties of the structure remain aligned around bounded consequence, sufficient time, preserved flexibility, and contained propagation.

This leads to a further reframing: stability is not an achievement. It is a maintained system condition. Achieved states imply completion. Maintained states imply ongoing work by the structure itself. Stability persists only while the system continues to support it through preserved margin, kept-open pathways of response, bounded dependency, and sufficient absorptive depth. Once those conditions begin to narrow, stability may continue appearing present for a time, but its persistence becomes more conditional. The system remains stable only so long as the structural conditions that sustain stability remain active.

This creates the distinction between achieved state and maintained state. An achieved state is assumed to remain in place unless some external event disrupts it. A maintained state can decay internally if its supporting conditions are not continuously preserved. Controlled stability belongs to the second category. Structural conditions evolve even during calm periods. Buffers are consumed and replenished unevenly. Dependency weights shift. Timing assumptions tighten. Confidence in observed consistency encourages narrower tolerances. If stability is treated as achieved rather than maintained, these changes become harder to see because the system interprets current calm as proof of durable safety.

The implication is that stability decays if not actively maintained. This does not mean every period of calm produces immediate decline. It means that the structure supporting stability requires ongoing preservation if exposure is not to drift into more dangerous forms. Stability persists only while the system continues to support it. Once the supporting architecture narrows, continuity may still look intact for a while, but it is resting on thinner conditions than before. This is why calm periods are often the wrong times to infer permanence. They are precisely the times when exposure can become less visible while remaining active.

The illusion of permanent stability grows from this mismatch between observed consistency and structural robustness. Systems often interpret past stability as evidence of future reliability. Repeated calm periods reinforce confidence because nothing has recently broken, nothing has visibly propagated, and prior assumptions appear validated by the continuity of outcomes. But repetition of calm is not proof of durable resilience. It is only proof that recent conditions have stayed inside the structure's current tolerances. If those tolerances have narrowed beneath the surface, then repeated calm can increase confidence precisely while the system becomes more exposed.

This is the distinction between observed consistency and structural robustness. Consistency refers to the visible repetition of acceptable outcomes. Robustness refers to the deeper ability of the structure to continue producing such outcomes when conditions worsen. The two often move together during calm periods, but not necessarily. Apparent consistency can persist while concentration rises, while reliance on timing precision increases, while exposures become more correlated, or while flexibility is slowly traded for efficiency. Stability can therefore become most fragile when it appears most reliable, because confidence rises as exposure becomes less visible.

This false confidence is structurally important because it encourages tighter configurations. When nothing has gone wrong for some time, the system often concludes that its existing structure is stronger than it actually is. It may reduce slack, increase dependency concentration, narrow buffers, or rely more heavily on support conditions that have not yet been tested under adverse states. In this way, the appearance of permanent stability can help create the conditions under which stability becomes less durable. The problem is not confidence as an attitude. The problem is confidence as a misreading of calm-state evidence.

Controlled stability therefore depends on limitation rather than expansion. Control does not emerge from maximizing output, widening exposure, or adding complexity for its own sake. It emerges from bounding consequence, constraining propagation, and preserving enough capacity that the system can continue functioning when conditions change. The relevant distinction is between expansion and constraint. Expansion seeks more throughput, more output, or more reach, often by allowing more continuity to depend on fewer highly utilized points. Constraint limits how much exposure any one node, pathway, or layer is allowed to carry.

This matters because systems do not fail from insufficient growth in any direct mechanical sense. They fail from unbounded exposure. Growth or complexity may coexist with stability if consequence remains bounded, but where expansion increases concentration, reduces margin, compresses timing, or weakens protective depth, it undermines the very conditions that make continuity possible. Control is therefore achieved through what is prevented, not merely through what is added. The most important features of controlled stability are often the ones that limit how far disruption can travel, how large loss can become, and how quickly time can disappear once instability begins.

Limitation is structurally productive because it preserves capacity. It keeps local failures local enough, maintains enough remaining room for response, and prevents single points of weakness from governing the whole structure. Expansion that outruns limitation creates fragility because it enlarges the amount of continuity attached to failure-prone channels without preserving the bounds required to keep those channels from becoming decisive. Stability therefore belongs more naturally to systems that preserve limits than to systems that assume continuous enlargement can substitute for structural control.

The chapter resolves into a final synthesis. Exposure is constant. Risk persists whether or not outcomes are currently adverse. Structure determines whether that exposure remains inside survivable bounds or develops into propagated instability. Stability exists only within maintained limits. It is not permanent, self-sustaining, or guaranteed by past calm. It is conditional, structural, and continuously maintained. The system remains stable only while it continues containing what it cannot eliminate, preserving time where pressure would otherwise compress it, and ensuring that disruption does not acquire the scale or speed required to overwhelm continuity.

Stability is not something a system achieves once—it is something a system must continuously sustain by containing what it cannot eliminate.

About the Author

Mark Ellison writes about structural durability in systems exposed to volatility.

His work focuses on long-horizon stability across financial architecture, career positioning, cognitive resilience, and physical capacity. Rather than treating these domains as separate disciplines, he approaches them as interdependent systems governed by load, margin, buffer depth, and threshold behavior.

The Stability framework examines how fragility accumulates gradually and how disciplined structural calibration preserves optionality across decades. The objective is not optimization for peak outcomes, but preservation of functional continuity under variance.

Money Stability is part of a broader multi-domain stability ecosystem developed under Perennial Publishing, each domain addressing a distinct vector of long-term durability.

The work is designed for readers who prefer structural clarity over motivational rhetoric and long-horizon coherence over short-term intensity.

The Money Stability Series

Money Stability: *How to Build Financial Control in an Unstable World* (Cornerstone Volume)

Liquidity and Runway: *How to Build Financial Time, Extend Your Runway, and Stay Stable in an Unstable Economy*

Income Stability: *How to Build Predictable, Durable, and Resilient Income*

Expense Stability: *How to Control Spending, Reduce Leakage, and Create Consistency*

Risk Stability: *How to Control Exposure, Limit Downside, and Stay Financially Stable*

Future titles expand the Money Stability framework:

Governance Stability
Financial Stability

Part of a Broader Stability Framework

The Money Stability Series is part of a larger stability ecosystem published by Perennial Publishing.

Related domains include:

Metabolic Stability — biological load, energy, and recovery capacity

Career Stability — income durability, positioning, and transition resilience

Mental Stability — cognitive steadiness under pressure and uncertainty

Emotional Stability — regulatory steadiness in environments that do not slow down

Each domain approaches stability as a structural problem: capacity versus load, buffers versus shocks, and governance versus drift. Together, they form a unified framework for long-horizon durability across the major systems that determine life trajectory.

About Perennial Publishing

Perennial Publishing produces practical systems guides for building stability in an unstable world.

Our books explore the foundations of long-term resilience across health, finance, career, and everyday decision-making. Each title focuses on clear frameworks, durable principles, and practical strategies that help readers build lasting stability rather than short-term fixes.

The Perennial catalog includes series on metabolic health, financial stability, career systems, and personal consistency. While each book stands on its own, they share a common goal: helping individuals create durable systems that support a stable and sustainable life.

Made in the USA
Monee, IL
12 November 2026

20727d12-21ae-4597-b4d1-fa5beddb98ceR01